55 Turkey Recipes for Home

By: Kelly Johnson

Table of Contents

- Classic Roast Turkey
- Herb-Rubbed Thanksgiving Turkey
- Citrus and Herb Grilled Turkey
- Smoked Turkey with Maple Glaze
- Cranberry Glazed Turkey Breast
- Cajun-Spiced Roast Turkey
- Lemon-Honey Glazed Turkey Legs
- Teriyaki Turkey Skewers
- Pesto-Roasted Turkey Thighs
- Garlic and Rosemary Turkey Roast
- Apple Cider Brined Turkey
- Balsamic and Dijon Glazed Turkey Breast
- Maple Bourbon Glazed Turkey
- Turkey and Stuffing Casserole
- Bacon-Wrapped Turkey Tenderloin
- Mediterranean Stuffed Turkey Breast
- Southwestern Turkey Chili
- Grilled Turkey Burgers with Avocado
- Turkey and Wild Rice Soup
- Asian-Inspired Turkey Meatballs
- Turkey Enchiladas with Salsa Verde
- BBQ Pulled Turkey Sandwiches
- Turkey and Cranberry Quesadillas
- Thai Turkey Lettuce Wraps
- Turkey and Vegetable Stir-Fry
- Creamy Turkey and Mushroom Risotto
- Turkey and Spinach Stuffed Shells
- Turkey and Sweet Potato Curry
- Greek Turkey Souvlaki
- Turkey and Quinoa Salad with Pomegranate
- Turkey and Broccoli Alfredo
- Moroccan Spiced Turkey Tagine
- Turkey Pot Pie with Flaky Crust
- Teriyaki Turkey Rice Bowls
- Turkey and Black Bean Chili

- Turkey and Cornbread Stuffing Muffins
- Turkey and Cranberry Sliders
- Turkey and Sweet Potato Hash
- Turkey Taco Lettuce Wraps
- Turkey and Cranberry Pesto Panini
- Turkey and Mushroom Stroganoff
- Turkey and Cranberry Pizza
- Turkey and Butternut Squash Tacos
- Turkey and Sage Sausage Stuffing
- Turkey and Vegetable Kabobs
- Turkey and Cranberry Croissant Sandwiches
- Turkey and Spinach Frittata
- Turkey and Green Bean Stir-Fry
- Turkey and Cranberry Wontons
- Turkey and Cheddar Stuffed Peppers
- Turkey and Cranberry Stuffed Acorn Squash
- Turkey and Pesto Pasta Salad
- Turkey and Brussels Sprouts Skillet
- Turkey and Cranberry Empanadas
- Turkey and Cranberry Hand Pies

Classic Roast Turkey

Ingredients:

- 1 whole turkey (12-14 pounds)
- Salt and pepper, to taste
- 1 cup unsalted butter, softened
- 1 tablespoon chopped fresh herbs (thyme, rosemary, sage)
- 1 onion, quartered
- 1 lemon, halved
- 1 head of garlic, halved
- 4 cups chicken or turkey broth
- 1/2 cup dry white wine (optional)
- 1/4 cup all-purpose flour (for gravy)

Instructions:

Preheat your oven to 325°F (165°C). Place the oven rack in the lower third of the oven.

Remove the turkey from the refrigerator and let it come to room temperature for about 1 hour.

Pat the turkey dry with paper towels, both inside and out.

Season the cavity with salt and pepper. Stuff it with the quartered onion, halved lemon, and halved garlic.

In a small bowl, mix together the softened butter and chopped fresh herbs.

Carefully loosen the skin over the turkey breast and spread half of the herb butter underneath the skin. Rub the remaining butter over the outside of the turkey.

Truss the turkey with kitchen twine, if desired, to help it cook evenly.

Place the turkey on a rack in a roasting pan, breast side up.

Pour the chicken or turkey broth into the bottom of the roasting pan. Optionally, add white wine for additional flavor.

Roast the turkey in the preheated oven. Baste every 30 minutes with pan juices and cover the turkey loosely with aluminum foil if the skin begins to brown too quickly.

Roast until the internal temperature reaches 165°F (74°C) in the thickest part of the thigh without touching the bone. This may take approximately 3 to 4 hours, depending on the size of the turkey.

Once done, transfer the turkey to a carving board, cover it with foil, and let it rest for at least 20 minutes before carving.

While the turkey rests, you can make gravy by combining pan drippings with flour over medium heat. Whisk until smooth and gradually add broth until the desired consistency is reached.

Carve and serve the Classic Roast Turkey with your favorite sides and gravy.

This Classic Roast Turkey recipe delivers a perfectly moist and flavorful bird with a golden brown skin. The combination of aromatic herbs and a simple preparation method makes it an excellent choice for your Thanksgiving or holiday feast.

Herb-Rubbed Thanksgiving Turkey

Ingredients:

- 1 whole turkey (14-16 pounds)
- Salt and black pepper, to taste
- 1 cup unsalted butter, softened
- 4 cloves garlic, minced
- 2 tablespoons fresh rosemary, chopped
- 2 tablespoons fresh thyme, chopped
- 2 tablespoons fresh sage, chopped
- Zest of 1 lemon
- 1 onion, quartered
- 1 lemon, quartered
- 4 cups chicken or turkey broth
- 1 cup dry white wine (optional)
- 1/4 cup all-purpose flour (for gravy)

Instructions:

Preheat your oven to 325°F (165°C). Place the oven rack in the lower third of the oven.

Remove the turkey from the refrigerator and allow it to come to room temperature for about 1 hour.

Pat the turkey dry with paper towels, both inside and out.

Season the cavity with salt and black pepper. Stuff it with the quartered onion and lemon.

In a bowl, combine the softened butter, minced garlic, chopped rosemary, thyme, sage, and lemon zest.

Carefully loosen the skin over the turkey breast and spread about 2/3 of the herb butter underneath the skin. Rub the remaining butter over the outside of the turkey.

Truss the turkey with kitchen twine, if desired, to help it cook evenly.

Place the turkey on a rack in a roasting pan, breast side up.

Pour the chicken or turkey broth into the bottom of the roasting pan. Optionally, add white wine for additional flavor.

Roast the turkey in the preheated oven. Baste every 30 minutes with pan juices and cover the turkey loosely with aluminum foil if the skin begins to brown too quickly.

Roast until the internal temperature reaches 165°F (74°C) in the thickest part of the thigh without touching the bone. This may take approximately 3.5 to 4.5 hours, depending on the size of the turkey.

Once done, transfer the turkey to a carving board, cover it with foil, and let it rest for at least 20 minutes before carving.

While the turkey rests, you can make gravy by combining pan drippings with flour over medium heat. Whisk until smooth and gradually add broth until the desired consistency is reached.

Carve and serve the Herb-Rubbed Thanksgiving Turkey with your favorite sides and gravy.

This Herb-Rubbed Thanksgiving Turkey is infused with aromatic herbs, garlic, and lemon, creating a flavorful and beautifully seasoned centerpiece for your holiday table. The herb-infused butter adds richness, and the slow roasting ensures a moist and succulent turkey. It's a delightful addition to your Thanksgiving feast or any special occasion.

Citrus and Herb Grilled Turkey

Ingredients:

- 1 whole turkey (12-14 pounds)
- Salt and black pepper, to taste
- 1 cup olive oil
- Zest of 2 lemons
- Zest of 2 oranges
- 1/4 cup fresh lemon juice
- 1/4 cup fresh orange juice
- 4 cloves garlic, minced
- 2 tablespoons fresh thyme, chopped
- 2 tablespoons fresh rosemary, chopped
- 2 tablespoons fresh sage, chopped
- 1 teaspoon paprika
- 1 teaspoon dried oregano
- 1 teaspoon ground cumin
- Wooden or metal skewers for trussing
- Citrus slices (lemons and oranges) for garnish

Instructions:

Preheat your grill to medium-high heat.
Remove the turkey from the refrigerator and let it come to room temperature for about 30 minutes.
Pat the turkey dry with paper towels, both inside and out.
Season the cavity with salt and black pepper.
In a bowl, whisk together olive oil, lemon zest, orange zest, lemon juice, orange juice, minced garlic, chopped thyme, rosemary, sage, paprika, oregano, and cumin to create the marinade.
Place the turkey on a cutting board, breast side up. Using your hands, carefully separate the skin from the breast without tearing it.
Rub a generous amount of the marinade underneath the turkey skin, ensuring even coverage.
Truss the turkey using skewers to secure the wings and legs.
Brush the outside of the turkey with the remaining marinade.
Place the turkey on the preheated grill, breast side up.

Grill the turkey over indirect heat, maintaining a consistent temperature of around 350°F (175°C). Cover the grill.

Grill until the internal temperature reaches 165°F (74°C) in the thickest part of the thigh without touching the bone. This may take approximately 2.5 to 3.5 hours, depending on the size of the turkey.

During the grilling process, baste the turkey with the remaining marinade every 30 minutes for added flavor.

Once done, transfer the grilled turkey to a cutting board, cover it with foil, and let it rest for at least 20 minutes before carving.

Garnish with citrus slices and serve the Citrus and Herb Grilled Turkey with your favorite sides.

This Citrus and Herb Grilled Turkey is a flavorful and succulent alternative to traditional roasted turkey. The citrus-infused marinade, combined with aromatic herbs, imparts a bright and zesty taste. Grilling adds a smoky depth, making it a perfect choice for outdoor gatherings or those looking to add a unique twist to their holiday feast.

Smoked Turkey with Maple Glaze

Ingredients:

- 1 whole turkey (12-14 pounds), thawed if frozen
- Salt and black pepper, to taste
- 1 cup maple syrup
- 1/2 cup unsalted butter, melted
- 1/4 cup apple cider vinegar
- 2 tablespoons Dijon mustard
- 1 tablespoon smoked paprika
- 1 teaspoon garlic powder
- 1 teaspoon onion powder
- 1 teaspoon dried thyme
- 1 teaspoon ground cinnamon
- Apple or cherry wood chips for smoking

Instructions:

Preheat your smoker to 225°F (107°C) using apple or cherry wood chips for added flavor.

Remove the turkey from the refrigerator and pat it dry with paper towels, both inside and out.

Season the cavity with salt and black pepper.

In a bowl, whisk together maple syrup, melted butter, apple cider vinegar, Dijon mustard, smoked paprika, garlic powder, onion powder, dried thyme, and ground cinnamon to create the maple glaze.

Place the turkey on a cutting board, breast side up.

Carefully lift the skin over the turkey breast and rub a generous amount of the maple glaze underneath the skin, ensuring even coverage.

Truss the turkey using kitchen twine to secure the wings and legs.

Brush the outside of the turkey with the remaining maple glaze.

Place the turkey on the smoker rack, breast side up.

Smoke the turkey at 225°F (107°C) until the internal temperature reaches 165°F (74°C) in the thickest part of the thigh without touching the bone. This may take approximately 5 to 6 hours, depending on the size of the turkey.

During the smoking process, baste the turkey with the maple glaze every 1-2 hours for additional flavor.

Once done, carefully transfer the smoked turkey to a cutting board, cover it with foil, and let it rest for at least 20 minutes before carving.
Serve the Smoked Turkey with Maple Glaze as a centerpiece for your holiday feast or any special occasion.

This Smoked Turkey with Maple Glaze offers a delightful combination of smoky flavors and sweet, maple-infused goodness. The slow smoking process enhances the turkey's natural juices, resulting in a tender and flavorful bird. The maple glaze adds a sweet and savory touch, making it a perfect choice for those who enjoy a unique and delicious twist on the traditional roasted turkey.

Cranberry Glazed Turkey Breast

Ingredients:

- 1 whole turkey breast (about 4-6 pounds), bone-in and skin-on
- Salt and black pepper, to taste
- 1 cup cranberry sauce (homemade or store-bought)
- 1/2 cup orange juice
- 1/4 cup honey
- 2 tablespoons Dijon mustard
- 1 tablespoon balsamic vinegar
- 1 teaspoon dried thyme
- 1 teaspoon garlic powder
- 1 teaspoon onion powder
- Orange zest for garnish (optional)

Instructions:

Preheat your oven to 350°F (175°C).
Pat the turkey breast dry with paper towels and season it with salt and black pepper.
In a saucepan over medium heat, combine cranberry sauce, orange juice, honey, Dijon mustard, balsamic vinegar, dried thyme, garlic powder, and onion powder. Stir well and let it simmer for about 5-7 minutes until it forms a glaze. Remove from heat.
Place the turkey breast in a roasting pan, skin side up.
Brush a generous amount of the cranberry glaze over the turkey breast, covering it evenly.
Roast the turkey breast in the preheated oven, basting with the cranberry glaze every 20-30 minutes, until the internal temperature reaches 165°F (74°C) in the thickest part of the meat. This may take approximately 1.5 to 2 hours, depending on the size of the turkey breast.
Once done, tent the turkey breast with aluminum foil and let it rest for about 15 minutes before carving.
Slice the turkey breast and drizzle with additional cranberry glaze.
Garnish with orange zest if desired.
Serve the Cranberry Glazed Turkey Breast as a flavorful and festive main dish for your holiday celebrations.

This Cranberry Glazed Turkey Breast brings a burst of fruity and tangy flavors to your holiday table. The combination of cranberry, orange, and honey creates a deliciously glazed turkey that's both sweet and savory. It's a perfect option for smaller gatherings or when you're looking for a turkey dish that stands out with vibrant and festive flavors.

Cajun-Spiced Roast Turkey

Ingredients:

- 1 whole turkey (12-14 pounds)
- Salt and black pepper, to taste
- 1/2 cup unsalted butter, melted
- 2 tablespoons Cajun seasoning
- 1 tablespoon paprika
- 1 tablespoon garlic powder
- 1 tablespoon onion powder
- 1 tablespoon dried thyme
- 1 tablespoon dried oregano
- 1 teaspoon cayenne pepper (adjust to taste)
- 1 lemon, quartered
- 1 onion, quartered
- 4 cloves garlic, smashed
- 1 cup chicken or turkey broth

Instructions:

Preheat your oven to 325°F (165°C).
Remove the turkey from the refrigerator and allow it to come to room temperature for about 1 hour.
Pat the turkey dry with paper towels, both inside and out.
Season the cavity with salt and black pepper.
In a small bowl, mix together melted butter, Cajun seasoning, paprika, garlic powder, onion powder, dried thyme, dried oregano, and cayenne pepper to create the Cajun spice rub.
Carefully separate the turkey skin from the breast using your hands. Rub a generous amount of the Cajun spice rub under the skin and all over the outside of the turkey.
Place the lemon, onion, and garlic cloves in the turkey cavity.
Truss the turkey with kitchen twine, if desired.
Place the turkey on a rack in a roasting pan, breast side up.
Pour the chicken or turkey broth into the bottom of the roasting pan.
Roast the turkey in the preheated oven. Baste with pan juices every 30 minutes, covering the turkey loosely with foil if the skin begins to brown too quickly.

Roast until the internal temperature reaches 165°F (74°C) in the thickest part of the thigh without touching the bone. This may take approximately 3.5 to 4.5 hours, depending on the size of the turkey.

Once done, transfer the turkey to a carving board, cover it with foil, and let it rest for at least 20 minutes before carving.

Serve the Cajun-Spiced Roast Turkey with your favorite sides for a flavorful and zesty twist on a classic roast turkey.

This Cajun-Spiced Roast Turkey brings a bold and spicy kick to your holiday table. The Cajun seasoning blend, with its combination of herbs and spices, adds depth and warmth to the turkey, creating a flavorful and aromatic dish. It's a perfect choice for those who enjoy a little heat and want to infuse their Thanksgiving or holiday meal with a Cajun-inspired twist.

Lemon-Honey Glazed Turkey Legs

Ingredients:

- 4 turkey legs
- Salt and black pepper, to taste
- 1/2 cup unsalted butter, melted
- 1/4 cup honey
- Zest of 2 lemons
- Juice of 2 lemons
- 3 cloves garlic, minced
- 1 tablespoon Dijon mustard
- 1 teaspoon dried thyme
- 1 teaspoon paprika
- 1/2 teaspoon cayenne pepper (adjust to taste)

Instructions:

Preheat your oven to 375°F (190°C).
Pat the turkey legs dry with paper towels and season them with salt and black pepper.
In a bowl, whisk together melted butter, honey, lemon zest, lemon juice, minced garlic, Dijon mustard, dried thyme, paprika, and cayenne pepper to create the glaze.
Place the turkey legs on a baking sheet lined with parchment paper or aluminum foil.
Brush the turkey legs generously with the lemon-honey glaze, ensuring even coverage.
Roast the turkey legs in the preheated oven for about 1 to 1.5 hours or until the internal temperature reaches 165°F (74°C) in the thickest part.
Baste the turkey legs with the glaze every 20-30 minutes during the roasting process.
For a caramelized finish, you can broil the turkey legs for the last 5-7 minutes, turning them occasionally to achieve a golden brown color.
Once done, remove the turkey legs from the oven and let them rest for a few minutes before serving.
Serve the Lemon-Honey Glazed Turkey Legs with additional glaze on the side for dipping.

These Lemon-Honey Glazed Turkey Legs offer a delightful combination of sweet and tangy flavors with a touch of citrusy brightness. The honey and lemon glaze creates a glossy, caramelized exterior, while the turkey remains juicy and tender on the inside. This dish is perfect for a festive dinner or a unique addition to your holiday table.

Teriyaki Turkey Skewers

Ingredients:

For the Teriyaki Marinade:

- 1/2 cup soy sauce
- 1/4 cup mirin (Japanese sweet rice wine)
- 2 tablespoons sake (Japanese rice wine)
- 2 tablespoons honey
- 2 cloves garlic, minced
- 1 teaspoon ginger, grated
- 1 tablespoon sesame oil
- 1 tablespoon cornstarch (optional, for thickening)

For the Turkey Skewers:

- 1 1/2 pounds turkey breast or turkey tenderloins, cut into 1-inch cubes
- Bell peppers, cut into chunks
- Red onion, cut into chunks
- Pineapple chunks
- Wooden skewers, soaked in water for at least 30 minutes

Instructions:

In a bowl, whisk together soy sauce, mirin, sake, honey, minced garlic, grated ginger, and sesame oil to make the teriyaki marinade. If you prefer a thicker sauce, you can add cornstarch by mixing it with a little water and stirring it into the marinade.

Place the turkey cubes in a resealable plastic bag or shallow dish. Pour half of the teriyaki marinade over the turkey, reserving the other half for later. Marinate the turkey in the refrigerator for at least 30 minutes, or preferably, up to 4 hours.

Preheat your grill or grill pan to medium-high heat.

Thread the marinated turkey cubes onto the soaked wooden skewers, alternating with bell peppers, red onion, and pineapple chunks.

Grill the turkey skewers for about 10-15 minutes, turning occasionally, until the turkey is cooked through and has a nice char on the edges.

While grilling, brush the skewers with the reserved teriyaki marinade to add extra flavor.

Once the turkey is cooked through (reaching an internal temperature of 165°F or 74°C), remove the skewers from the grill.
Serve the Teriyaki Turkey Skewers over rice or noodles, drizzling with any remaining teriyaki sauce and garnishing with sesame seeds and chopped green onions if desired.

These Teriyaki Turkey Skewers are a delicious fusion of Japanese flavors with grilled turkey, creating a perfect balance of sweet and savory. The teriyaki marinade not only adds depth to the turkey but also enhances the overall skewer experience. Enjoy these skewers as a delightful and flavorful main dish for your family or guests.

Pesto-Roasted Turkey Thighs

Ingredients:

- 4 turkey thighs, bone-in and skin-on
- Salt and black pepper, to taste
- 1 cup basil pesto (homemade or store-bought)
- 1 lemon, juiced
- 4 cloves garlic, minced
- 1/4 cup grated Parmesan cheese
- 2 tablespoons olive oil
- 1 teaspoon dried oregano
- 1/2 teaspoon red pepper flakes (optional)
- Fresh basil leaves for garnish (optional)

Instructions:

Preheat your oven to 375°F (190°C).
Pat the turkey thighs dry with paper towels and season them with salt and black pepper.
In a bowl, mix together basil pesto, lemon juice, minced garlic, grated Parmesan cheese, olive oil, dried oregano, and red pepper flakes (if using).
Place the turkey thighs on a baking sheet lined with parchment paper or aluminum foil.
Brush the turkey thighs generously with the pesto mixture, ensuring even coverage.
Roast the turkey thighs in the preheated oven for about 45-60 minutes or until the internal temperature reaches 165°F (74°C) in the thickest part.
During the roasting process, you can baste the turkey thighs with any drippings or additional pesto mixture for added flavor.
Once done, remove the turkey thighs from the oven and let them rest for a few minutes before serving.
Garnish with fresh basil leaves if desired.
Serve the Pesto-Roasted Turkey Thighs with your favorite sides, such as roasted vegetables, mashed potatoes, or a simple salad.

These Pesto-Roasted Turkey Thighs offer a burst of vibrant flavors from the basil pesto, creating a juicy and aromatic dish. The combination of herbs, garlic, and Parmesan adds depth to the turkey, while the roasting process ensures a crispy skin and succulent meat. It's a delightful option for a family dinner or a special occasion where you want to elevate the flavors of traditional roasted turkey.

Garlic and Rosemary Turkey Roast

Ingredients:

- 1 whole turkey (12-14 pounds)
- Salt and black pepper, to taste
- 1/2 cup unsalted butter, softened
- 6 cloves garlic, minced
- 2 tablespoons fresh rosemary, chopped
- Zest of 1 lemon
- 2 tablespoons olive oil
- 1 lemon, sliced
- 1 onion, sliced
- 4 cups chicken or turkey broth

Instructions:

Preheat your oven to 325°F (165°C). Place the oven rack in the lower third of the oven.
Remove the turkey from the refrigerator and let it come to room temperature for about 1 hour.
Pat the turkey dry with paper towels, both inside and out.
Season the cavity with salt and black pepper.
In a bowl, mix together softened butter, minced garlic, chopped rosemary, and lemon zest.
Carefully loosen the skin over the turkey breast and spread half of the garlic and rosemary butter underneath the skin. Rub the remaining butter over the outside of the turkey.
Truss the turkey with kitchen twine, if desired, to help it cook evenly.
Rub the olive oil over the turkey skin and season the outside with additional salt and black pepper.
Place the turkey on a rack in a roasting pan, breast side up.
Scatter lemon slices and onion slices around the turkey in the roasting pan.
Pour the chicken or turkey broth into the bottom of the roasting pan.
Roast the turkey in the preheated oven. Baste every 30 minutes with pan juices and cover the turkey loosely with aluminum foil if the skin begins to brown too quickly.

Roast until the internal temperature reaches 165°F (74°C) in the thickest part of the thigh without touching the bone. This may take approximately 3.5 to 4.5 hours, depending on the size of the turkey.
Once done, transfer the turkey to a carving board, cover it with foil, and let it rest for at least 20 minutes before carving.
Serve the Garlic and Rosemary Turkey Roast with your favorite sides and enjoy the flavorful, herb-infused roast.

This Garlic and Rosemary Turkey Roast is a classic yet flavorful option for your holiday or special occasion meal. The combination of garlic, rosemary, and lemon adds aromatic richness to the turkey, creating a mouthwatering roast that's sure to be a hit with your family and guests.

Apple Cider Brined Turkey

Ingredients:

For the Brine:

- 1 gallon (4 quarts) apple cider
- 1 cup kosher salt
- 1 cup brown sugar
- 1 tablespoon whole black peppercorns
- 1 tablespoon whole allspice berries
- 1 tablespoon whole cloves
- 4 sprigs fresh rosemary
- 4 sprigs fresh thyme
- 2 large bay leaves
- 1 orange, sliced
- 1 lemon, sliced

For the Turkey:

- 1 whole turkey (12-14 pounds), thawed if frozen
- 4 cups cold water
- 1 onion, quartered
- 1 apple, quartered
- 4 sprigs fresh rosemary
- 4 sprigs fresh thyme
- 1 cup chicken or turkey broth (for basting)

Instructions:

In a large stockpot, combine the apple cider, kosher salt, brown sugar, black peppercorns, allspice berries, cloves, rosemary, thyme, bay leaves, orange slices, and lemon slices. Bring the mixture to a boil, stirring to dissolve the salt and sugar. Allow the brine to cool completely.

Remove the giblets and neck from the turkey cavity. Rinse the turkey under cold water and pat it dry with paper towels.

Place the turkey in a large brining bag or a food-safe brining container.

Pour the cooled brine over the turkey, ensuring it is fully submerged. Seal the bag or cover the container and place it in the refrigerator for 12 to 24 hours.

Preheat your oven to 325°F (165°C).

Remove the turkey from the brine and rinse it under cold water. Pat it dry with paper towels.

In a large roasting pan, place the turkey on a rack. Add 4 cups of cold water to the bottom of the pan.

Stuff the turkey cavity with quartered onion, quartered apple, fresh rosemary, and fresh thyme.

Tie the turkey legs together with kitchen twine and tuck the wings under the body.

Roast the turkey in the preheated oven. Baste every 30 minutes with chicken or turkey broth and the pan juices. If the skin begins to brown too quickly, cover the turkey loosely with aluminum foil.

Roast until the internal temperature reaches 165°F (74°C) in the thickest part of the thigh without touching the bone. This may take approximately 3.5 to 4.5 hours, depending on the size of the turkey.

Once done, transfer the turkey to a carving board, cover it with foil, and let it rest for at least 20 minutes before carving.

Serve the Apple Cider Brined Turkey with your favorite sides for a moist and flavorful Thanksgiving centerpiece.

This Apple Cider Brined Turkey offers a juicy and flavorful twist to your Thanksgiving feast. The combination of apple cider, aromatic spices, and herbs in the brine infuses the turkey with a delightful taste. Roasting the turkey with additional aromatics enhances the overall flavor, creating a delicious and memorable holiday meal.

Balsamic and Dijon Glazed Turkey Breast

Ingredients:

For the Glaze:

- 1/2 cup balsamic vinegar
- 1/4 cup Dijon mustard
- 1/4 cup honey
- 2 tablespoons olive oil
- 2 cloves garlic, minced
- 1 teaspoon dried thyme
- Salt and black pepper, to taste

For the Turkey Breast:

- 1 bone-in turkey breast (about 4-6 pounds)
- Salt and black pepper, to taste
- 2 tablespoons olive oil
- Fresh thyme sprigs for garnish (optional)

Instructions:

Preheat your oven to 375°F (190°C).
In a small saucepan over medium heat, combine balsamic vinegar, Dijon mustard, honey, olive oil, minced garlic, dried thyme, salt, and black pepper. Bring the mixture to a simmer, stirring frequently. Reduce heat and let it simmer for about 5-7 minutes until the glaze thickens slightly. Remove from heat.
Pat the turkey breast dry with paper towels. Season it with salt and black pepper.
In a skillet, heat olive oil over medium-high heat. Brown the turkey breast on all sides, about 3-4 minutes per side.
Transfer the turkey breast to a roasting pan, skin side up.
Brush the turkey breast with the balsamic and Dijon glaze, covering it evenly.
Roast the turkey breast in the preheated oven for about 1 to 1.5 hours, or until the internal temperature reaches 165°F (74°C) in the thickest part.
Baste the turkey breast with the glaze every 20-30 minutes during the roasting process.
Once done, remove the turkey breast from the oven and let it rest for about 15 minutes before carving.

Garnish with fresh thyme sprigs if desired.
Carve the Balsamic and Dijon Glazed Turkey Breast and serve it with additional glaze on the side.

This Balsamic and Dijon Glazed Turkey Breast is a delicious and elegant option for a smaller Thanksgiving or holiday meal. The combination of balsamic vinegar, Dijon mustard, and honey creates a sweet and tangy glaze that enhances the natural flavors of the turkey. It's a flavorful and beautiful centerpiece that's sure to impress your guests.

Maple Bourbon Glazed Turkey

Ingredients:

For the Glaze:

- 1 cup pure maple syrup
- 1/2 cup bourbon
- 1/4 cup unsalted butter
- 2 tablespoons Dijon mustard
- 1 tablespoon soy sauce
- 1 tablespoon Worcestershire sauce
- 1 teaspoon garlic powder
- Salt and black pepper, to taste

For the Turkey:

- 1 whole turkey (12-14 pounds), thawed if frozen
- Salt and black pepper, to taste
- 1 onion, quartered
- 1 apple, quartered
- 4 sprigs fresh rosemary
- 4 sprigs fresh thyme
- 1 cup chicken or turkey broth

Instructions:

Preheat your oven to 325°F (165°C).
In a saucepan over medium heat, combine maple syrup, bourbon, butter, Dijon mustard, soy sauce, Worcestershire sauce, garlic powder, salt, and black pepper. Bring the mixture to a simmer, stirring frequently. Let it simmer for about 5-7 minutes until the glaze thickens slightly. Remove from heat.
Remove the giblets and neck from the turkey cavity. Rinse the turkey under cold water and pat it dry with paper towels.
Season the cavity with salt and black pepper.
Place the turkey on a rack in a roasting pan, breast side up.
Stuff the turkey cavity with quartered onion, quartered apple, fresh rosemary, and fresh thyme.
Truss the turkey with kitchen twine, if desired.

Pour the chicken or turkey broth into the bottom of the roasting pan.
Brush the turkey with the maple bourbon glaze, covering it evenly.
Roast the turkey in the preheated oven. Baste every 30 minutes with pan juices and cover the turkey loosely with foil if the skin begins to brown too quickly.
Roast until the internal temperature reaches 165°F (74°C) in the thickest part of the thigh without touching the bone. This may take approximately 3.5 to 4.5 hours, depending on the size of the turkey.
Once done, transfer the turkey to a carving board, cover it with foil, and let it rest for at least 20 minutes before carving.
Serve the Maple Bourbon Glazed Turkey with additional glaze on the side for drizzling.

This Maple Bourbon Glazed Turkey brings a rich and flavorful twist to your Thanksgiving or holiday table. The combination of sweet maple syrup, robust bourbon, and savory seasonings creates a mouthwatering glaze that enhances the natural juices of the turkey. It's a perfect choice for those who enjoy a touch of sweetness and warmth in their holiday feast.

Turkey and Stuffing Casserole

Ingredients:

For the Casserole:

- 4 cups cooked turkey, shredded or diced
- 4 cups prepared stuffing
- 2 cups green beans, cooked and cut into bite-sized pieces
- 1 cup sliced mushrooms (optional)
- 1 cup shredded cheddar cheese

For the Creamy Sauce:

- 1/4 cup unsalted butter
- 1/4 cup all-purpose flour
- 2 cups turkey or chicken broth
- 1 cup milk
- Salt and black pepper, to taste
- 1 teaspoon dried thyme
- 1 teaspoon dried sage

Instructions:

Preheat your oven to 350°F (175°C).
In a large mixing bowl, combine the cooked turkey, prepared stuffing, green beans, sliced mushrooms (if using), and shredded cheddar cheese. Mix well and transfer the mixture to a greased casserole dish.
In a saucepan over medium heat, melt the butter. Add the flour and whisk continuously to create a roux. Cook for 1-2 minutes until it becomes golden brown.
Slowly pour in the turkey or chicken broth while whisking to avoid lumps. Add the milk, dried thyme, dried sage, salt, and black pepper. Continue whisking until the sauce thickens, about 5-7 minutes.
Pour the creamy sauce over the turkey and stuffing mixture in the casserole dish. Ensure the sauce coats the ingredients evenly.

Bake the casserole in the preheated oven for 25-30 minutes or until it is heated through and bubbly.

If desired, you can broil the casserole for an additional 2-3 minutes to achieve a golden brown top.

Remove from the oven and let it cool slightly before serving.

Serve the Turkey and Stuffing Casserole as a comforting and hearty dish, perfect for using leftover Thanksgiving turkey.

This Turkey and Stuffing Casserole is a wonderful way to repurpose Thanksgiving leftovers into a comforting and delicious meal. The combination of turkey, stuffing, green beans, and a creamy sauce creates a satisfying casserole that captures the flavors of the holiday season. It's a convenient and tasty option for making the most of your Thanksgiving feast.

Bacon-Wrapped Turkey Tenderloin

Ingredients:

- 2 turkey tenderloins
- Salt and black pepper, to taste
- 1 teaspoon garlic powder
- 1 teaspoon onion powder
- 1 teaspoon smoked paprika
- 1 teaspoon dried thyme
- 8-10 slices of bacon
- 2 tablespoons olive oil
- 1 tablespoon Dijon mustard
- 2 tablespoons maple syrup

Instructions:

Preheat your oven to 375°F (190°C).
Season the turkey tenderloins with salt, black pepper, garlic powder, onion powder, smoked paprika, and dried thyme. Rub the seasoning evenly over the tenderloins.
Lay out the bacon slices on a cutting board or a flat surface, slightly overlapping.
Place a turkey tenderloin at the end of the bacon slices and wrap the bacon around it, covering the entire surface. Repeat with the second tenderloin.
In a skillet over medium-high heat, heat olive oil. Add the bacon-wrapped turkey tenderloins and sear them on all sides until the bacon is golden brown.
In a small bowl, mix Dijon mustard and maple syrup.
Transfer the seared turkey tenderloins to a baking dish and brush them with the Dijon mustard and maple syrup mixture.
Bake in the preheated oven for 25-30 minutes or until the internal temperature reaches 165°F (74°C) in the thickest part of the turkey.
If desired, you can broil the bacon-wrapped turkey for an additional 2-3 minutes to crisp up the bacon.
Remove from the oven and let it rest for a few minutes before slicing.
Slice the Bacon-Wrapped Turkey Tenderloin and serve it with your favorite sides.

This Bacon-Wrapped Turkey Tenderloin combines the succulence of turkey with the rich and smoky flavor of bacon. The Dijon mustard and maple syrup glaze add a sweet and tangy element, making it a delicious and visually appealing dish. It's a perfect choice for a special dinner or when you want to elevate your turkey game.

Mediterranean Stuffed Turkey Breast

Ingredients:

For the Turkey Breast:

- 1 boneless, skinless turkey breast (about 2 pounds)
- Salt and black pepper, to taste
- 1 tablespoon olive oil
- 1 teaspoon dried oregano
- 1 teaspoon dried thyme

For the Stuffing:

- 1 cup spinach, chopped
- 1/2 cup sun-dried tomatoes, chopped
- 1/2 cup Kalamata olives, pitted and chopped
- 1/2 cup feta cheese, crumbled
- 2 cloves garlic, minced
- 1 tablespoon olive oil
- Salt and black pepper, to taste

Instructions:

Preheat your oven to 375°F (190°C).
Butterfly the turkey breast by slicing it horizontally, but not cutting all the way through, and then open it like a book. Pound the turkey breast gently to an even thickness.
Season the inside of the turkey breast with salt, black pepper, dried oregano, and dried thyme.
In a skillet over medium heat, heat olive oil. Add minced garlic and cook for about 1 minute until fragrant.
Add chopped spinach to the skillet and cook until wilted.
In a bowl, combine the wilted spinach, chopped sun-dried tomatoes, chopped Kalamata olives, crumbled feta cheese, and olive oil. Season with salt and black pepper to taste. Mix well.
Spread the stuffing mixture evenly over the inside of the turkey breast.
Roll the turkey breast tightly, starting from one end, to encase the stuffing. Use kitchen twine to secure the roll at intervals.

Place the rolled and tied turkey breast on a baking sheet or in a roasting pan.
Rub the outside of the turkey breast with olive oil and sprinkle with additional salt, black pepper, dried oregano, and dried thyme.

Roast in the preheated oven for about 1 to 1.5 hours or until the internal temperature reaches 165°F (74°C) in the thickest part.

Allow the Mediterranean Stuffed Turkey Breast to rest for about 10 minutes before slicing.

Slice and serve the stuffed turkey breast with any remaining stuffing and your favorite sides.

This Mediterranean Stuffed Turkey Breast is a flavorful and elegant dish that brings the tastes of the Mediterranean to your table. The combination of spinach, sun-dried tomatoes, Kalamata olives, and feta cheese creates a delicious stuffing, while the turkey breast remains moist and tender. It's a perfect option for a festive meal or a special occasion.

Southwestern Turkey Chili

Ingredients:

- 1 pound ground turkey
- 1 tablespoon olive oil
- 1 onion, diced
- 2 bell peppers (any color), diced
- 3 cloves garlic, minced
- 1 can (15 ounces) black beans, drained and rinsed
- 1 can (15 ounces) kidney beans, drained and rinsed
- 1 can (15 ounces) diced tomatoes
- 1 cup corn kernels (fresh or frozen)
- 1 cup chicken broth
- 2 tablespoons tomato paste
- 1 tablespoon chili powder
- 1 teaspoon ground cumin
- 1 teaspoon smoked paprika
- 1/2 teaspoon dried oregano
- Salt and black pepper, to taste
- Optional toppings: shredded cheese, sour cream, chopped green onions, cilantro

Instructions:

In a large pot or Dutch oven, heat olive oil over medium heat. Add ground turkey and cook until browned, breaking it apart with a spoon as it cooks.

Add diced onion, bell peppers, and minced garlic to the pot. Cook until vegetables are softened, about 5 minutes.

Stir in tomato paste, chili powder, ground cumin, smoked paprika, dried oregano, salt, and black pepper. Cook for an additional 2 minutes to allow the spices to toast and become fragrant.

Add black beans, kidney beans, diced tomatoes (with their juice), corn kernels, and chicken broth to the pot. Stir to combine.

Bring the chili to a simmer, then reduce the heat to low. Cover and let it simmer for at least 30 minutes to allow the flavors to meld together.

Taste and adjust the seasoning as needed. If you prefer a spicier chili, you can add more chili powder or a dash of cayenne pepper.

Serve the Southwestern Turkey Chili hot, topped with shredded cheese, a dollop of sour cream, chopped green onions, and cilantro if desired.

Enjoy the chili on its own or with your favorite accompaniments, such as cornbread or tortilla chips.

This Southwestern Turkey Chili is a hearty and flavorful dish that combines lean ground turkey with a mix of beans, vegetables, and spices. It's a perfect one-pot meal for a cozy dinner or a gathering with friends. Customize the toppings to your liking for a delicious and satisfying chili experience.

Grilled Turkey Burgers with Avocado

Ingredients:

For the Turkey Patties:

- 1.5 pounds ground turkey
- 1/2 cup breadcrumbs
- 1/4 cup grated Parmesan cheese
- 1/4 cup finely chopped red onion
- 2 cloves garlic, minced
- 1 tablespoon Worcestershire sauce
- 1 teaspoon dried oregano
- 1 teaspoon dried thyme
- Salt and black pepper, to taste

For Grilling and Serving:

- Olive oil, for brushing the grill
- 4 whole-grain burger buns
- 1 avocado, sliced
- Lettuce leaves
- Tomato slices
- Red onion rings
- Optional condiments: mayonnaise, Dijon mustard

Instructions:

Preheat your grill to medium-high heat.
In a large mixing bowl, combine ground turkey, breadcrumbs, grated Parmesan, chopped red onion, minced garlic, Worcestershire sauce, dried oregano, dried thyme, salt, and black pepper. Mix until well combined.
Divide the turkey mixture into 4 equal portions and shape them into patties.
Brush the grill grates with olive oil to prevent sticking.
Place the turkey patties on the preheated grill and cook for about 5-6 minutes per side, or until the internal temperature reaches 165°F (74°C) and the burgers are cooked through.
In the last few minutes of cooking, you can place the whole-grain buns on the grill to toast them lightly.

Assemble the burgers by placing a turkey patty on each bun. Top with sliced avocado, lettuce leaves, tomato slices, and red onion rings.
Add condiments of your choice, such as mayonnaise or Dijon mustard.
Serve the Grilled Turkey Burgers with Avocado alongside your favorite side dishes.

These Grilled Turkey Burgers with Avocado offer a lean and flavorful alternative to traditional beef burgers. The addition of Parmesan, red onion, and herbs enhances the turkey patties, while the creamy avocado adds a delightful freshness. Whether you're looking for a healthier option or simply craving a tasty burger, this recipe is sure to satisfy your appetite.

Turkey and Wild Rice Soup

Ingredients:

- 1 cup wild rice, uncooked
- 1 pound cooked turkey, shredded or diced
- 1 onion, diced
- 2 carrots, diced
- 2 celery stalks, diced
- 2 cloves garlic, minced
- 8 cups turkey or chicken broth
- 1 teaspoon dried thyme
- 1 teaspoon dried rosemary
- 1 bay leaf
- Salt and black pepper, to taste
- 1/2 cup all-purpose flour
- 1/2 cup unsalted butter
- 2 cups whole milk
- 1 cup half-and-half
- Fresh parsley, chopped (for garnish)

Instructions:

Cook the wild rice according to the package instructions. Set aside.
In a large pot or Dutch oven, melt the butter over medium heat. Add diced onion, carrots, celery, and minced garlic. Sauté until the vegetables are softened, about 5 minutes.
Sprinkle the flour over the vegetables and stir well to coat. Cook for an additional 2-3 minutes to remove the raw flour taste.
Gradually whisk in the turkey or chicken broth, ensuring there are no lumps. Add the dried thyme, dried rosemary, bay leaf, salt, and black pepper. Bring the mixture to a simmer.
Add the cooked turkey and cooked wild rice to the pot. Simmer for about 15-20 minutes, allowing the flavors to meld together.
In a separate saucepan, heat the whole milk and half-and-half until warm but not boiling.
Slowly pour the warm milk mixture into the soup, stirring continuously. Continue simmering for an additional 10-15 minutes.
Adjust the seasoning to taste, and discard the bay leaf.

Ladle the Turkey and Wild Rice Soup into bowls. Garnish with chopped fresh parsley.
Serve the soup hot, and enjoy the comforting flavors of this hearty turkey and wild rice creation.

This Turkey and Wild Rice Soup is a comforting and wholesome way to use leftover turkey. The combination of wild rice, vegetables, and a creamy broth creates a satisfying soup that's perfect for chilly days or as a post-Thanksgiving treat. Feel free to customize the herbs and vegetables based on your preferences.

Asian-Inspired Turkey Meatballs

Ingredients:

For the Meatballs:

- 1 pound ground turkey
- 1/2 cup breadcrumbs
- 1/4 cup green onions, finely chopped
- 2 cloves garlic, minced
- 1 tablespoon fresh ginger, grated
- 1 tablespoon soy sauce
- 1 tablespoon hoisin sauce
- 1 teaspoon sesame oil
- 1 egg, beaten
- Salt and black pepper, to taste
- Sesame seeds, for garnish (optional)
- Chopped cilantro, for garnish (optional)

For the Sauce:

- 1/4 cup soy sauce
- 2 tablespoons hoisin sauce
- 1 tablespoon rice vinegar
- 1 tablespoon honey
- 1 teaspoon sesame oil
- 1 teaspoon fresh ginger, grated
- 1 clove garlic, minced

Instructions:

Preheat your oven to 400°F (200°C). Line a baking sheet with parchment paper.
In a large mixing bowl, combine ground turkey, breadcrumbs, chopped green onions, minced garlic, grated ginger, soy sauce, hoisin sauce, sesame oil, beaten egg, salt, and black pepper. Mix until well combined.
Shape the mixture into meatballs, about 1 to 1.5 inches in diameter, and place them on the prepared baking sheet.
Bake in the preheated oven for 15-20 minutes or until the meatballs are cooked through and browned on the outside.

While the meatballs are baking, prepare the sauce. In a small saucepan, combine soy sauce, hoisin sauce, rice vinegar, honey, sesame oil, grated ginger, and minced garlic. Heat over medium heat, stirring occasionally, until the sauce thickens slightly.

Once the meatballs are done, transfer them to a serving dish. Pour the sauce over the meatballs, ensuring they are well-coated.

Garnish the Asian-Inspired Turkey Meatballs with sesame seeds and chopped cilantro if desired.

Serve the meatballs over rice, noodles, or as an appetizer with toothpicks for a delicious and flavorful dish.

These Asian-Inspired Turkey Meatballs are packed with savory and umami flavors. The combination of soy sauce, hoisin sauce, and fresh ginger adds a delicious twist to traditional meatballs. Whether served as an appetizer or part of a main course, these meatballs are sure to be a hit with their bold and enticing taste.

Turkey Enchiladas with Salsa Verde

Ingredients:

For the Enchiladas:

- 2 cups cooked turkey, shredded
- 1 cup black beans, drained and rinsed
- 1 cup corn kernels (fresh, frozen, or canned)
- 1 cup shredded Monterey Jack cheese
- 1/2 cup diced red onion
- 1/4 cup chopped fresh cilantro
- 8-10 small flour tortillas

For the Salsa Verde:

- 2 cups salsa verde (store-bought or homemade)
- 1/2 cup sour cream
- 1 teaspoon ground cumin
- Salt and black pepper, to taste

For Topping:

- 1 cup shredded cheddar cheese
- Sliced jalapeños (optional)
- Chopped fresh cilantro
- Lime wedges

Instructions:

Preheat your oven to 375°F (190°C). Grease a baking dish.
In a mixing bowl, combine shredded turkey, black beans, corn, Monterey Jack cheese, diced red onion, and chopped cilantro. Mix well.
In a separate bowl, whisk together salsa verde, sour cream, ground cumin, salt, and black pepper.
Spoon a small amount of the salsa verde mixture into the bottom of the prepared baking dish.
Assemble the enchiladas: Spoon the turkey and vegetable mixture onto each flour tortilla, roll them up, and place them seam side down in the baking dish.
Pour the remaining salsa verde mixture over the top of the enchiladas.

Sprinkle shredded cheddar cheese over the enchiladas.
Bake in the preheated oven for 20-25 minutes, or until the cheese is melted and bubbly.
Remove from the oven and let it cool slightly before serving.
Garnish the Turkey Enchiladas with Salsa Verde with sliced jalapeños, chopped cilantro, and lime wedges.
Serve the enchiladas hot and enjoy the delicious combination of flavors.

These Turkey Enchiladas with Salsa Verde are a tasty way to use leftover turkey in a Mexican-inspired dish. The combination of shredded turkey, black beans, corn, and cheese is rolled up in flour tortillas and baked with a zesty salsa verde and sour cream sauce. It's a flavorful and comforting dish that's perfect for a family dinner or when you're craving a bit of Southwestern flair.

Turkey and Cranberry Quesadillas

Ingredients:

- 2 cups cooked turkey, shredded
- 1 cup cranberry sauce
- 1 cup shredded Monterey Jack cheese
- 1 cup shredded cheddar cheese
- 1/4 cup chopped green onions
- 1/4 cup chopped fresh cilantro
- 4 large flour tortillas
- 2 tablespoons butter or olive oil, for cooking

Instructions:

In a bowl, mix together the shredded turkey, cranberry sauce, Monterey Jack cheese, cheddar cheese, chopped green onions, and chopped cilantro until well combined.
Heat a large skillet or griddle over medium heat.
Place a flour tortilla on the skillet and spoon a portion of the turkey and cranberry mixture onto half of the tortilla.
Fold the other half of the tortilla over the filling, creating a half-moon shape.
Press down gently with a spatula and cook for 2-3 minutes on each side, or until the tortilla is golden brown and the cheese is melted.
Repeat the process for the remaining tortillas and filling.
Remove the quesadillas from the skillet and let them cool for a minute before slicing.
Slice each quesadilla into wedges and serve warm.
Optionally, garnish with additional chopped cilantro and serve with extra cranberry sauce for dipping.
Enjoy these Turkey and Cranberry Quesadillas as a delicious way to use leftover turkey in a festive and flavorful dish!

These Turkey and Cranberry Quesadillas are a creative and tasty way to repurpose leftover Thanksgiving turkey. The combination of tender turkey, sweet cranberry sauce, and gooey melted cheese makes for a delightful and satisfying quesadilla. Perfect for a quick meal or as a fun appetizer during the holiday season!

Thai Turkey Lettuce Wraps

Ingredients:

For the Turkey Filling:

- 1 lb ground turkey
- 1 tbsp vegetable oil
- 2 cloves garlic, minced
- 1 tbsp ginger, grated
- 1 red bell pepper, finely diced
- 1 carrot, julienned
- 1/2 cup water chestnuts, chopped
- 3 green onions, chopped
- 1/4 cup fresh cilantro, chopped
- 2 tbsp soy sauce
- 1 tbsp fish sauce
- 1 tbsp oyster sauce
- 1 tbsp lime juice
- 1 tsp brown sugar
- Salt and pepper, to taste

For Serving:

- Bibb or iceberg lettuce leaves
- Lime wedges
- Crushed peanuts
- Sriracha sauce (optional)

Instructions:

Heat vegetable oil in a skillet over medium heat. Sauté minced garlic and grated ginger for 1 minute.

Add ground turkey to the skillet and cook until browned.

Stir in diced red bell pepper, julienned carrot, and chopped water chestnuts. Cook for 2-3 minutes until vegetables are tender.

In a small bowl, whisk together soy sauce, fish sauce, oyster sauce, lime juice, brown sugar, salt, and pepper.
Pour the sauce over the turkey mixture and cook for an additional 2-3 minutes.
Remove from heat and stir in chopped green onions and cilantro.
Spoon the Thai turkey mixture into lettuce leaves.
Garnish with crushed peanuts and a squeeze of lime juice. Add Sriracha sauce for heat if desired.
Serve immediately and enjoy these light and flavorful Thai Turkey Lettuce Wraps!

These wraps are a perfect blend of savory, crunchy, and fresh flavors, making them a delightful dish for any meal.

Turkey and Vegetable Stir-Fry

Ingredients:

For the Stir-Fry:

- 1 lb turkey breast or ground turkey
- 2 tablespoons soy sauce
- 1 tablespoon oyster sauce
- 1 tablespoon hoisin sauce
- 1 tablespoon cornstarch
- 2 tablespoons vegetable oil, divided
- 3 cups mixed vegetables (broccoli florets, bell peppers, snap peas, carrots, etc.), chopped
- 3 cloves garlic, minced
- 1 tablespoon fresh ginger, grated
- Salt and pepper, to taste
- Sesame seeds and chopped green onions for garnish (optional)

For the Sauce:

- 1/4 cup low-sodium soy sauce
- 2 tablespoons oyster sauce
- 1 tablespoon hoisin sauce
- 1 tablespoon rice vinegar
- 1 tablespoon sesame oil

Instructions:

In a bowl, mix the turkey with soy sauce, oyster sauce, hoisin sauce, and cornstarch. Let it marinate for about 15-20 minutes.

Heat 1 tablespoon of vegetable oil in a wok or large skillet over medium-high heat. Add the marinated turkey and cook until browned and cooked through. Remove the turkey from the wok and set aside.

In the same wok, add another tablespoon of vegetable oil. Add minced garlic and grated ginger, sauté for about 30 seconds until fragrant.

Add the mixed vegetables to the wok and stir-fry for 3-5 minutes until they are crisp-tender.

In a small bowl, whisk together the sauce ingredients: soy sauce, oyster sauce, hoisin sauce, rice vinegar, and sesame oil.

Return the cooked turkey to the wok with the vegetables. Pour the sauce over the mixture and toss everything together until well coated and heated through.

Season with salt and pepper to taste.

Garnish with sesame seeds and chopped green onions if desired.

Serve the Turkey and Vegetable Stir-Fry over rice or noodles.

This Turkey and Vegetable Stir-Fry is a quick and flavorful dish that's perfect for a weeknight dinner. It's a versatile recipe, so feel free to customize the vegetables based on your preferences. Enjoy the delicious blend of savory turkey, crisp vegetables, and a flavorful sauce!

Creamy Turkey and Mushroom Risotto

Ingredients:

- 1 lb turkey breast, cooked and shredded
- 1 1/2 cups Arborio rice
- 1 cup mushrooms, sliced
- 1 onion, finely chopped
- 2 cloves garlic, minced
- 4 cups chicken or turkey broth, kept warm
- 1 cup dry white wine
- 1/2 cup Parmesan cheese, grated
- 1/4 cup unsalted butter
- 2 tablespoons olive oil
- Salt and pepper, to taste
- Fresh parsley, chopped (for garnish)

Instructions:

In a large skillet or Dutch oven, heat the olive oil over medium heat. Add the onions and sauté until they are soft and translucent.

Add the mushrooms to the skillet and cook until they release their moisture and become golden brown.

Stir in the minced garlic and Arborio rice. Cook for 1-2 minutes until the rice is lightly toasted.

Pour in the white wine and cook until it's mostly absorbed by the rice.

Begin adding the warm broth, one ladle at a time, stirring continuously. Allow each ladle of broth to be mostly absorbed before adding the next. Continue this process until the rice is creamy and cooked to al dente texture. This will take about 18-20 minutes.

Stir in the shredded turkey and cook for an additional 2-3 minutes until the turkey is heated through.

Remove the skillet from heat and stir in the Parmesan cheese and butter. Season with salt and pepper to taste.

Garnish the Creamy Turkey and Mushroom Risotto with chopped fresh parsley. Serve the risotto warm, and enjoy the rich and comforting flavors!

This Creamy Turkey and Mushroom Risotto is a comforting and satisfying dish that makes the most of leftover turkey. The combination of creamy Arborio rice, tender turkey, and earthy mushrooms creates a delightful meal. The white wine adds depth to the flavors, and the Parmesan cheese brings a luxurious creaminess to the dish. Perfect for a special dinner or whenever you crave a hearty and creamy risotto!

Turkey and Spinach Stuffed Shells

Ingredients:

- 1 lb large pasta shells
- 1 lb ground turkey
- 1 small onion, finely chopped
- 2 cloves garlic, minced
- 1 cup frozen chopped spinach, thawed and drained
- 1 cup ricotta cheese
- 1 cup mozzarella cheese, shredded
- 1/2 cup Parmesan cheese, grated
- 1 egg, beaten
- 2 cups marinara sauce
- Salt and pepper, to taste
- Fresh basil or parsley, chopped (for garnish)

Instructions:

Preheat the oven to 350°F (175°C).
Cook the pasta shells according to the package instructions. Drain and set aside.
In a skillet over medium heat, cook the ground turkey until browned. Add chopped onion and minced garlic, and cook until the onion is softened. Season with salt and pepper.
In a large bowl, combine the cooked turkey mixture, thawed and drained spinach, ricotta cheese, half of the mozzarella cheese, half of the Parmesan cheese, and beaten egg. Mix well.
Stuff each cooked pasta shell with the turkey and spinach mixture.
Spread a thin layer of marinara sauce in the bottom of a baking dish.
Arrange the stuffed shells in the baking dish. Pour the remaining marinara sauce over the shells.
Sprinkle the remaining mozzarella and Parmesan cheese over the top.
Cover the baking dish with aluminum foil and bake in the preheated oven for 25-30 minutes, or until the cheese is melted and bubbly.
Remove the foil and bake for an additional 5-10 minutes until the cheese is golden and slightly crispy.
Garnish with chopped fresh basil or parsley before serving.

Serve the Turkey and Spinach Stuffed Shells hot, and enjoy this comforting and flavorful dish!

These Turkey and Spinach Stuffed Shells are a delicious twist on classic stuffed shells, incorporating lean ground turkey and nutritious spinach. The cheesy and savory filling combined with marinara sauce makes for a comforting and satisfying dish that's perfect for family dinners or special occasions.

Turkey and Sweet Potato Curry

Ingredients:

- 1 lb ground turkey
- 2 large sweet potatoes, peeled and diced
- 1 onion, finely chopped
- 3 cloves garlic, minced
- 1 tablespoon ginger, grated
- 1 can (14 oz) diced tomatoes
- 1 can (14 oz) coconut milk
- 2 tablespoons red curry paste
- 1 teaspoon ground turmeric
- 1 teaspoon ground cumin
- 1 teaspoon ground coriander
- 1 teaspoon paprika
- Salt and pepper, to taste
- 2 tablespoons vegetable oil
- Fresh cilantro, chopped (for garnish)
- Cooked rice or naan (for serving)

Instructions:

In a large skillet or pot, heat vegetable oil over medium heat. Add chopped onion and cook until softened.

Add minced garlic and grated ginger to the skillet, sautéing for about 1 minute until fragrant.

Add ground turkey to the skillet and cook until browned, breaking it apart with a spoon.

Stir in red curry paste, ground turmeric, ground cumin, ground coriander, and paprika. Cook for an additional 2-3 minutes to allow the spices to release their flavors.

Add diced sweet potatoes to the skillet and mix well.

Pour in the diced tomatoes and coconut milk. Season with salt and pepper to taste. Stir the mixture thoroughly.

Bring the curry to a simmer, then reduce the heat to low, cover, and let it cook for about 15-20 minutes or until the sweet potatoes are tender.

Taste and adjust the seasoning if needed.

Serve the Turkey and Sweet Potato Curry over cooked rice or with naan. Garnish with chopped fresh cilantro before serving.

Enjoy the rich and flavorful Turkey and Sweet Potato Curry, a hearty and comforting meal!

This Turkey and Sweet Potato Curry offers a delightful blend of aromatic spices, lean ground turkey, and sweet potatoes for a hearty and comforting dish. The combination of coconut milk and tomatoes adds a creamy and savory element, making it a perfect choice for a satisfying dinner. Serve it over rice or with naan for a complete and delicious meal.

Greek Turkey Souvlaki

Ingredients:

For the Turkey Marinade:

- 1 lb turkey breast, cut into bite-sized pieces
- 1/4 cup olive oil
- 3 tablespoons Greek yogurt
- 3 cloves garlic, minced
- 1 teaspoon dried oregano
- 1 teaspoon dried thyme
- 1 teaspoon smoked paprika
- Juice of 1 lemon
- Salt and pepper, to taste

For Tzatziki Sauce:

- 1 cup Greek yogurt
- 1 cucumber, grated and drained
- 2 cloves garlic, minced
- 1 tablespoon fresh dill, chopped
- 1 tablespoon olive oil
- Salt and pepper, to taste

For Serving:

- Pita bread
- Cherry tomatoes, halved
- Red onion, thinly sliced
- Fresh lettuce or arugula
- Feta cheese, crumbled (optional)

Instructions:

In a bowl, mix together all the marinade ingredients for the turkey: olive oil, Greek yogurt, minced garlic, dried oregano, dried thyme, smoked paprika, lemon juice, salt, and pepper.

Add the turkey pieces to the marinade, ensuring they are well-coated. Cover and refrigerate for at least 30 minutes, or preferably, marinate overnight for enhanced flavor.

While the turkey is marinating, prepare the tzatziki sauce. In a bowl, combine Greek yogurt, grated and drained cucumber, minced garlic, chopped fresh dill, olive oil, salt, and pepper. Mix well and refrigerate until ready to serve.

Thread the marinated turkey pieces onto skewers.

Preheat a grill or grill pan over medium-high heat. Grill the turkey skewers for about 5-7 minutes per side, or until cooked through and slightly charred.

Warm the pita bread on the grill for a minute on each side.

Assemble the souvlaki by placing the grilled turkey off the skewers onto the warm pita bread.

Top with cherry tomatoes, sliced red onion, fresh lettuce or arugula, and crumbled feta cheese if desired.

Drizzle with tzatziki sauce.

Serve the Greek Turkey Souvlaki immediately and enjoy this delicious and flavorful Greek-inspired dish!

This Greek Turkey Souvlaki is a tasty and healthy option for a satisfying meal. The marinated turkey, grilled to perfection, combined with the freshness of vegetables and the creaminess of tzatziki sauce, creates a delightful Mediterranean-inspired experience. Serve it in warm pita bread for an authentic touch or over a bed of salad for a lighter option.

Turkey and Quinoa Salad with Pomegranate

Ingredients:

For the Salad:

- 1 cup cooked quinoa, cooled
- 1 lb turkey breast, cooked and diced
- 1 cup cucumber, diced
- 1 cup cherry tomatoes, halved
- 1/2 cup red onion, finely chopped
- 1/2 cup feta cheese, crumbled
- 1/2 cup fresh parsley, chopped
- 1/2 cup pomegranate arils

For the Dressing:

- 1/4 cup olive oil
- 2 tablespoons balsamic vinegar
- 1 tablespoon honey
- 1 teaspoon Dijon mustard
- Salt and pepper, to taste

Instructions:

In a large salad bowl, combine the cooked quinoa, diced turkey, cucumber, cherry tomatoes, red onion, feta cheese, and fresh parsley.

In a small bowl, whisk together the dressing ingredients: olive oil, balsamic vinegar, honey, Dijon mustard, salt, and pepper.

Drizzle the dressing over the salad and toss gently to combine, ensuring all ingredients are well coated.

Sprinkle pomegranate arils over the top of the salad for a burst of sweetness and color.

Refrigerate the Turkey and Quinoa Salad for at least 30 minutes before serving to allow the flavors to meld.

Serve chilled and enjoy this wholesome and flavorful Turkey and Quinoa Salad with Pomegranate!

This Turkey and Quinoa Salad with Pomegranate is a nutritious and vibrant dish that combines the lean protein of turkey with the goodness of quinoa and fresh vegetables. The addition of pomegranate arils not only adds a delightful burst of sweetness but also contributes antioxidants and a pop of color. The honey-balsamic dressing ties all the flavors together, creating a delicious and satisfying salad. Perfect for a light lunch or a refreshing dinner option!

Turkey and Broccoli Alfredo

Ingredients:

- 8 oz fettuccine pasta
- 1 lb turkey breast, cooked and sliced
- 2 cups broccoli florets, blanched
- 2 tablespoons unsalted butter
- 2 cloves garlic, minced
- 1 cup heavy cream
- 1 cup grated Parmesan cheese
- Salt and black pepper, to taste
- Fresh parsley, chopped (for garnish)

Instructions:

Cook the fettuccine pasta according to the package instructions. Drain and set aside.
In a large skillet, melt the butter over medium heat. Add minced garlic and sauté until fragrant.
Add the sliced turkey to the skillet and cook for a few minutes to warm through.
Stir in the blanched broccoli florets and cook for an additional 2-3 minutes.
Pour in the heavy cream and bring the mixture to a simmer. Allow it to simmer for 2-3 minutes.
Gradually add the grated Parmesan cheese to the skillet, stirring constantly, until the cheese is melted and the sauce is smooth.
Season the Alfredo sauce with salt and black pepper to taste.
Add the cooked fettuccine pasta to the skillet, tossing to coat the pasta evenly with the sauce.
Continue to cook for a few more minutes until the pasta is heated through.
Remove the skillet from heat and garnish with chopped fresh parsley.
Serve the Turkey and Broccoli Alfredo immediately, and enjoy this creamy and comforting dish!

This Turkey and Broccoli Alfredo is a comforting and flavorful twist on the classic Alfredo pasta, incorporating lean turkey and nutritious broccoli. The rich and creamy Alfredo sauce, made with Parmesan cheese and heavy cream, coats the fettuccine pasta and turkey, creating a satisfying and indulgent dish. It's a quick and easy recipe for a delicious weeknight dinner.

Moroccan Spiced Turkey Tagine

Ingredients:

- 1.5 lbs turkey thighs, bone-in and skinless, cut into pieces
- 2 tablespoons olive oil
- 1 large onion, finely chopped
- 3 cloves garlic, minced
- 1 teaspoon ground cumin
- 1 teaspoon ground coriander
- 1 teaspoon ground cinnamon
- 1 teaspoon paprika
- 1/2 teaspoon ground ginger
- 1/2 teaspoon ground turmeric
- 1/2 teaspoon cayenne pepper (adjust to taste)
- Salt and black pepper, to taste
- 1 can (14 oz) diced tomatoes
- 1/2 cup dried apricots, chopped
- 1/4 cup green olives, pitted and sliced
- 1 cup chicken broth
- Fresh cilantro, chopped (for garnish)
- Cooked couscous (for serving)

Instructions:

In a large, heavy-bottomed pot or tagine, heat the olive oil over medium-high heat.
Add the chopped onions and sauté until they become translucent.
Add minced garlic and continue to sauté for another minute until fragrant.
Place the turkey pieces in the pot and brown them on all sides.
In a small bowl, mix together the ground cumin, coriander, cinnamon, paprika, ground ginger, turmeric, cayenne pepper, salt, and black pepper.
Sprinkle the spice mixture over the turkey and stir well to coat.
Pour in the diced tomatoes, chicken broth, chopped apricots, and sliced olives. Stir to combine.
Bring the mixture to a boil, then reduce the heat to low, cover, and simmer for about 1.5 to 2 hours or until the turkey is tender and cooked through.
Check the seasoning and adjust salt and pepper if needed.
Serve the Moroccan Spiced Turkey Tagine over cooked couscous.

Garnish with chopped fresh cilantro before serving.
Enjoy this flavorful and aromatic Moroccan Spiced Turkey Tagine, a dish that beautifully blends savory, sweet, and spicy flavors!

This Moroccan Spiced Turkey Tagine is a delightful dish that brings together the rich flavors of North African cuisine. The combination of aromatic spices, tender turkey, and the sweetness of apricots creates a flavorful and satisfying meal. Serve it over couscous to soak up the delicious sauce, and garnish with fresh cilantro for a burst of freshness. Perfect for a special dinner with a touch of exotic flair!

Turkey Pot Pie with Flaky Crust

Ingredients:

For the Filling:

- 2 cups cooked turkey, shredded or diced
- 2 tablespoons unsalted butter
- 1 onion, finely chopped
- 2 carrots, diced
- 2 celery stalks, diced
- 1 cup frozen peas
- 1/3 cup all-purpose flour
- 2 cups chicken or turkey broth
- 1 cup milk
- Salt and black pepper, to taste
- 1 teaspoon dried thyme
- 1 teaspoon dried rosemary

For the Crust:

- 2 1/2 cups all-purpose flour
- 1 cup unsalted butter, cold and cut into small cubes
- 1/2 cup ice water
- 1 teaspoon salt

Instructions:

For the Filling:

In a large skillet, melt the butter over medium heat. Add the chopped onion, carrots, and celery. Sauté until the vegetables are softened.
Stir in the flour to create a roux. Cook for 1-2 minutes to remove the raw flour taste.
Gradually whisk in the chicken or turkey broth and milk, ensuring there are no lumps. Cook until the mixture thickens.
Add the shredded or diced turkey, frozen peas, dried thyme, dried rosemary, salt, and black pepper. Stir to combine. Remove from heat and set aside.

For the Crust:

In a large mixing bowl, combine the flour and salt.

Add the cold, cubed butter to the flour mixture. Use a pastry cutter or your fingers to cut the butter into the flour until the mixture resembles coarse crumbs.

Gradually add the ice water, a few tablespoons at a time, and mix until the dough just comes together.

Divide the dough in half and shape each half into a disk. Wrap each disk in plastic wrap and refrigerate for at least 30 minutes.

Assembly:

Preheat the oven to 425°F (220°C).

Roll out one of the chilled dough disks on a floured surface to fit the bottom of your pie dish.

Place the rolled-out dough in the bottom of the pie dish.

Pour the turkey filling over the crust in the pie dish.

Roll out the second dough disk and place it over the filling. Trim and crimp the edges to seal the pie.

Cut a few slits in the top crust to allow steam to escape.

Bake in the preheated oven for 30-35 minutes or until the crust is golden brown and the filling is bubbly.

Allow the Turkey Pot Pie to cool for a few minutes before serving.

Slice, serve, and enjoy the comforting goodness of Turkey Pot Pie with a flaky crust!

This Turkey Pot Pie with a flaky crust is a classic and comforting dish that makes the most of leftover turkey. The rich and savory filling, surrounded by a golden and buttery crust, creates a delicious meal perfect for cozy dinners. The combination of tender turkey, colorful vegetables, and aromatic herbs makes this pot pie a family favorite.

Teriyaki Turkey Rice Bowls

Ingredients:

For the Teriyaki Sauce:

- 1/2 cup soy sauce
- 1/4 cup water
- 2 tablespoons honey
- 1 tablespoon rice vinegar
- 1 teaspoon sesame oil
- 1 teaspoon ginger, minced
- 1 teaspoon garlic, minced
- 1 tablespoon cornstarch mixed with 2 tablespoons water (to thicken)

For the Bowl:

- 1 lb turkey breast, thinly sliced
- 2 cups cooked jasmine rice
- 1 cup broccoli florets, steamed
- 1 carrot, julienned
- 1 green onion, sliced
- Sesame seeds (for garnish)
- Fresh cilantro or parsley (for garnish)
- Red pepper flakes (optional, for spice)

Instructions:

In a small saucepan, combine soy sauce, water, honey, rice vinegar, sesame oil, minced ginger, and minced garlic over medium heat. Bring the mixture to a simmer.

In a small bowl, mix cornstarch with water to create a slurry. Slowly whisk the slurry into the simmering sauce to thicken it. Continue simmering until the sauce reaches the desired thickness. Remove from heat and set aside.

In a skillet or wok, heat a bit of oil over medium-high heat. Add the thinly sliced turkey and cook until browned and cooked through.

Pour the teriyaki sauce over the cooked turkey in the skillet. Toss to coat the turkey in the sauce.

In serving bowls, assemble the rice bowls by placing a portion of cooked jasmine rice in each bowl.
Top the rice with teriyaki turkey slices, steamed broccoli florets, julienned carrots, and sliced green onions.
Drizzle extra teriyaki sauce over the bowls as desired.
Garnish with sesame seeds, fresh cilantro or parsley, and red pepper flakes if you like some heat.
Serve the Teriyaki Turkey Rice Bowls immediately and enjoy this delicious and flavorful Asian-inspired dish!

These Teriyaki Turkey Rice Bowls are a quick and delicious meal option that combines the savory and sweet flavors of teriyaki with tender slices of turkey and fresh vegetables. The homemade teriyaki sauce adds a delightful touch to the dish, and you can customize the toppings to your liking. It's a wholesome and satisfying meal perfect for busy weeknights.

Turkey and Black Bean Chili

Ingredients:

- 1 lb ground turkey
- 1 tablespoon olive oil
- 1 onion, diced
- 3 cloves garlic, minced
- 1 bell pepper, diced (any color)
- 1 can (15 oz) black beans, drained and rinsed
- 1 can (14 oz) diced tomatoes
- 1 can (6 oz) tomato paste
- 2 cups chicken broth
- 2 teaspoons chili powder
- 1 teaspoon cumin
- 1 teaspoon smoked paprika
- 1/2 teaspoon oregano
- 1/2 teaspoon cayenne pepper (adjust to taste)
- Salt and black pepper, to taste
- Fresh cilantro, chopped (for garnish)
- Shredded cheese, sour cream, and sliced green onions (optional, for serving)

Instructions:

In a large pot or Dutch oven, heat olive oil over medium heat. Add diced onions and sauté until softened.

Add minced garlic and diced bell pepper to the pot. Sauté for an additional 2-3 minutes until the vegetables are tender.

Add ground turkey to the pot and cook until browned, breaking it apart with a spoon.

Stir in chili powder, cumin, smoked paprika, oregano, and cayenne pepper. Cook for 1-2 minutes until the spices are fragrant.

Pour in diced tomatoes, tomato paste, black beans, and chicken broth. Stir well to combine.

Season the chili with salt and black pepper to taste. Bring the mixture to a simmer.

Reduce the heat to low, cover the pot, and let the chili simmer for at least 30 minutes to allow the flavors to meld. Stir occasionally.

Taste and adjust the seasoning if needed.
Serve the Turkey and Black Bean Chili hot, garnished with chopped cilantro.
Optionally, serve with shredded cheese, sour cream, and sliced green onions on top.
Enjoy this hearty and flavorful Turkey and Black Bean Chili on its own or with your favorite toppings!

This Turkey and Black Bean Chili is a delicious and nutritious option for a cozy and satisfying meal. Packed with protein from ground turkey and black beans, and flavored with a blend of spices, this chili is perfect for warming up on chilly days. Customize the toppings according to your preference, and serve it with a side of cornbread for a complete and comforting experience.

Turkey and Cornbread Stuffing Muffins

Ingredients:

For the Cornbread:

- 1 cup yellow cornmeal
- 1 cup all-purpose flour
- 1 tablespoon sugar
- 1 tablespoon baking powder
- 1/2 teaspoon salt
- 1 cup milk
- 1/4 cup unsalted butter, melted
- 1 large egg

For the Stuffing:

- 1 lb ground turkey
- 1 onion, finely chopped
- 2 celery stalks, finely chopped
- 2 cloves garlic, minced
- 1 teaspoon poultry seasoning
- Salt and black pepper, to taste
- 1/2 cup chicken broth
- 2 eggs, beaten

Instructions:

For the Cornbread:

Preheat the oven to 425°F (220°C). Grease a muffin tin or line it with paper liners.
In a large bowl, whisk together the cornmeal, flour, sugar, baking powder, and salt.
In another bowl, whisk together the milk, melted butter, and egg.
Pour the wet ingredients into the dry ingredients and stir until just combined.
Divide the cornbread batter evenly among the muffin cups.
Bake for 15-20 minutes or until the tops are golden brown and a toothpick inserted into the center comes out clean.
Allow the cornbread muffins to cool while you prepare the stuffing.

For the Stuffing:

In a skillet, cook the ground turkey over medium heat until browned. Drain any excess fat.

Add chopped onion, celery, and minced garlic to the skillet. Cook until the vegetables are softened.

Season the mixture with poultry seasoning, salt, and black pepper to taste.

Pour in the chicken broth and stir until well combined. Remove the skillet from heat.

In a large bowl, crumble the baked cornbread.

Add the cooked turkey and vegetable mixture to the bowl.

Beat the eggs and add them to the bowl. Mix everything together until well combined.

Preheat the oven to 350°F (175°C).

Grease the muffin tin or use paper liners again.

Spoon the cornbread stuffing mixture into the muffin cups.

Bake for 20-25 minutes or until the tops are golden brown.

Allow the Turkey and Cornbread Stuffing Muffins to cool slightly before serving.

Enjoy these delightful muffins as a tasty side dish for your Thanksgiving feast!

These Turkey and Cornbread Stuffing Muffins are a creative and convenient way to enjoy the classic flavors of Thanksgiving stuffing. The combination of moist cornbread and seasoned ground turkey, baked into individual portions, makes them perfect for holiday gatherings or any meal. They can be served alongside your favorite Thanksgiving dishes or enjoyed on their own with a dollop of gravy.

Turkey and Cranberry Sliders

Ingredients:

For the Sliders:

- 12 slider rolls
- 1 lb cooked turkey, thinly sliced
- 1 cup cranberry sauce
- 8 slices Swiss cheese
- 1/2 cup mayonnaise
- 1/4 cup Dijon mustard
- 1/4 cup unsalted butter, melted
- 1 tablespoon poppy seeds
- 1 tablespoon minced onion
- 1 tablespoon Worcestershire sauce

For the Topping:

- Fresh spinach leaves or arugula

Instructions:

Preheat the oven to 350°F (175°C).
Slice the slider rolls in half horizontally, keeping them connected.
Place the bottom half of the rolls in a baking dish.
In a small bowl, mix together mayonnaise and Dijon mustard. Spread the mixture evenly over the bottom half of the rolls.
Layer the thinly sliced turkey over the rolls.
Spoon cranberry sauce over the turkey.
Place Swiss cheese slices over the cranberry sauce.
Place the top half of the rolls over the cheese to close the sliders.
In another bowl, whisk together melted butter, poppy seeds, minced onion, and Worcestershire sauce.
Pour the butter mixture evenly over the sliders.
Cover the baking dish with aluminum foil and bake in the preheated oven for about 15-20 minutes or until the cheese is melted and the sliders are heated through.

Remove the foil and bake for an additional 5 minutes or until the tops are golden brown.
Remove from the oven and let them cool slightly.
Slice the sliders along the original lines to separate them.
Place a few fresh spinach leaves or arugula on each slider.
Serve the Turkey and Cranberry Sliders warm and enjoy this delightful combination of Thanksgiving flavors in a bite-sized treat!

These Turkey and Cranberry Sliders are a fantastic way to enjoy the flavors of Thanksgiving in a convenient and bite-sized form. The combination of tender turkey, cranberry sauce, and melted Swiss cheese, all baked into slider rolls, creates a delicious and satisfying appetizer or main dish. The addition of a Dijon-mayo spread and a poppy seed topping enhances the overall flavor profile. Perfect for holiday parties or as a creative way to use Thanksgiving leftovers!

Turkey and Sweet Potato Hash

Ingredients:

- 1 lb ground turkey
- 2 tablespoons olive oil
- 2 sweet potatoes, peeled and diced
- 1 bell pepper, diced
- 1 onion, diced
- 2 cloves garlic, minced
- 1 teaspoon ground cumin
- 1 teaspoon paprika
- 1/2 teaspoon chili powder
- Salt and black pepper, to taste
- 4 eggs (optional, for serving)
- Fresh cilantro, chopped (for garnish)

Instructions:

In a large skillet, heat olive oil over medium-high heat.
Add ground turkey to the skillet and cook until browned, breaking it apart with a spoon as it cooks.
Once the turkey is browned, add diced sweet potatoes, bell pepper, and onion to the skillet.
Sauté the mixture for 8-10 minutes or until the sweet potatoes are tender and the vegetables are cooked.
Add minced garlic, ground cumin, paprika, chili powder, salt, and black pepper to the skillet. Stir well to combine.
Continue to cook for an additional 2-3 minutes to allow the flavors to meld.
If desired, create four wells in the hash and crack an egg into each well. Cover the skillet and cook until the eggs are cooked to your liking.
Alternatively, you can cook the eggs separately and serve them on top of the hash.
Garnish with chopped fresh cilantro.
Serve the Turkey and Sweet Potato Hash warm and enjoy this flavorful and hearty dish for breakfast, brunch, or dinner!

This Turkey and Sweet Potato Hash is a delicious and wholesome dish that combines the savory goodness of ground turkey with the sweetness of sweet potatoes and a medley of vegetables. The aromatic spices add depth and warmth to the hash, creating a satisfying and nutritious meal. You can enjoy it on its own or topped with eggs for added protein. Perfect for a hearty breakfast or a quick and easy dinner option!

Turkey Taco Lettuce Wraps

Ingredients:

For the Turkey Taco Filling:

- 1 lb ground turkey
- 1 tablespoon olive oil
- 1 onion, finely chopped
- 2 cloves garlic, minced
- 1 packet taco seasoning (or use homemade seasoning)
- 1 cup tomato sauce
- 1/2 cup black beans, drained and rinsed
- 1/2 cup corn kernels (fresh or frozen)
- Salt and black pepper, to taste

For the Lettuce Wraps:

- Large lettuce leaves (such as iceberg or butter lettuce)
- Toppings: Diced tomatoes, shredded cheese, avocado slices, salsa, sour cream, chopped cilantro, lime wedges, etc.

Instructions:

For the Turkey Taco Filling:

In a large skillet, heat olive oil over medium-high heat.
Add chopped onion to the skillet and sauté until softened.
Add minced garlic and cook for another 1-2 minutes until fragrant.
Add ground turkey to the skillet and cook until browned, breaking it apart with a spoon as it cooks.
Stir in the taco seasoning and cook for a couple of minutes until well combined.
Pour in the tomato sauce and add black beans and corn. Mix well.
Season with salt and black pepper to taste. Simmer for 5-7 minutes until the mixture is heated through and flavors meld.
Remove from heat and set aside.

Assembling the Lettuce Wraps:

Wash and separate large lettuce leaves, creating cups for the filling.

Spoon the turkey taco filling into each lettuce cup.
Top with your favorite toppings, such as diced tomatoes, shredded cheese, avocado slices, salsa, sour cream, chopped cilantro, and a squeeze of lime.
Serve the Turkey Taco Lettuce Wraps immediately and enjoy this light and flavorful alternative to traditional tacos!

These Turkey Taco Lettuce Wraps offer a fresh and healthier twist to traditional tacos. The flavorful and seasoned ground turkey pairs perfectly with the crisp lettuce cups, and you can customize the toppings to suit your taste. It's a low-carb and gluten-free option that doesn't compromise on taste. Whether for lunch, dinner, or a quick snack, these lettuce wraps are a delightful and satisfying choice.

Turkey and Cranberry Pesto Panini

Ingredients:

For the Cranberry Pesto:

- 1 cup fresh cranberries
- 1/4 cup pine nuts
- 2 cloves garlic, minced
- 1 cup fresh basil leaves
- 1/2 cup grated Parmesan cheese
- 1/2 cup extra-virgin olive oil
- Salt and black pepper, to taste

For the Panini:

- Sliced turkey (leftover Thanksgiving turkey works great)
- Sourdough or ciabatta bread, sliced
- Provolone or Swiss cheese, sliced
- Butter (for grilling)

Instructions:

For the Cranberry Pesto:

In a food processor, combine fresh cranberries, pine nuts, minced garlic, fresh basil leaves, grated Parmesan cheese, and a pinch of salt.
Pulse the ingredients until well combined.
With the food processor running, slowly drizzle in the extra-virgin olive oil until the pesto reaches a smooth consistency.
Season with additional salt and black pepper to taste. Set aside.

For the Panini:

Preheat a panini press or grill pan.
Spread a generous layer of cranberry pesto on one side of each slice of bread.
Layer sliced turkey and cheese on half of the bread slices.

Top with the remaining slices of bread, pesto side down, to create sandwiches.
Lightly butter the outer sides of the sandwiches.
Place the sandwiches on the preheated panini press or grill pan.
Grill for 3-4 minutes, or until the bread is golden brown and the cheese is melted.
Carefully remove the panini from the press or pan.
Allow them to cool slightly before slicing.
Serve the Turkey and Cranberry Pesto Panini warm and enjoy the delicious combination of Thanksgiving flavors!

These Turkey and Cranberry Pesto Panini are a delightful way to enjoy the flavors of Thanksgiving in a sandwich. The cranberry pesto adds a burst of tartness and freshness, complementing the savory turkey and melted cheese. Grilling the panini gives the bread a crispy texture and brings all the flavors together. It's a perfect way to use leftover Thanksgiving turkey or to enjoy a taste of the holiday season any time of the year!

Turkey and Mushroom Stroganoff

Ingredients:

- 1 lb ground turkey
- 1 tablespoon olive oil
- 1 onion, finely chopped
- 2 cloves garlic, minced
- 8 oz mushrooms, sliced
- 2 tablespoons all-purpose flour
- 1 cup beef or vegetable broth
- 1 tablespoon Worcestershire sauce
- 1 teaspoon Dijon mustard
- 1/2 cup sour cream
- Salt and black pepper, to taste
- Fresh parsley, chopped (for garnish)
- Egg noodles or rice (for serving)

Instructions:

In a large skillet, heat olive oil over medium-high heat.
Add chopped onion to the skillet and sauté until softened.
Add minced garlic and sliced mushrooms to the skillet. Cook until the mushrooms are browned and any liquid has evaporated.
Push the mushrooms to the side of the skillet and add ground turkey. Cook until browned, breaking it apart with a spoon as it cooks.
Sprinkle flour over the turkey and mushrooms. Stir well to combine.
Pour in the broth, Worcestershire sauce, and Dijon mustard. Stir continuously to avoid lumps from forming.
Allow the mixture to simmer and thicken for 5-7 minutes.
Reduce the heat to low and stir in sour cream. Cook for an additional 2-3 minutes until the stroganoff is heated through.
Season with salt and black pepper to taste.
Serve the Turkey and Mushroom Stroganoff over egg noodles or rice.
Garnish with chopped fresh parsley.
Enjoy this creamy and flavorful Turkey and Mushroom Stroganoff as a comforting and satisfying meal!

This Turkey and Mushroom Stroganoff is a quick and delicious twist on the classic beef stroganoff. Ground turkey provides a lighter alternative, while the mushrooms add a savory depth to the dish. The creamy sauce, flavored with Worcestershire sauce and Dijon mustard, makes this stroganoff rich and satisfying. Serve it over egg noodles or rice for a complete and comforting meal that the whole family will enjoy.

Turkey and Cranberry Pizza

Ingredients:

For the Pizza Dough:

- 1 pound pizza dough (store-bought or homemade)

For the Pizza Toppings:

- 1 cup cooked turkey, shredded (leftover Thanksgiving turkey works well)
- 1/2 cup cranberry sauce
- 1 cup shredded mozzarella cheese
- 1/2 cup crumbled feta cheese
- 1/4 cup chopped red onion
- 1/4 cup chopped fresh cilantro or parsley
- Olive oil (for brushing)

Optional Garnish:

- Arugula tossed in balsamic vinaigrette

Instructions:

Preheat your oven according to the pizza dough instructions or to 475°F (245°C).
Roll out the pizza dough on a floured surface to your desired thickness.
Transfer the rolled-out dough to a pizza stone or a baking sheet lined with parchment paper.
Brush the dough with olive oil.
Spread the shredded turkey evenly over the pizza dough.
Spoon dollops of cranberry sauce over the turkey.
Sprinkle the shredded mozzarella and crumbled feta cheese over the toppings.
Distribute chopped red onion over the cheese.
Bake in the preheated oven for 12-15 minutes or until the crust is golden and the cheese is melted and bubbly.
Remove the pizza from the oven and sprinkle chopped cilantro or parsley over the top.
If desired, toss arugula in balsamic vinaigrette and place it on the pizza after baking.
Slice the Turkey and Cranberry Pizza and serve hot.

Enjoy this unique and delicious pizza that captures the flavors of Thanksgiving!

This Turkey and Cranberry Pizza is a creative and tasty way to use Thanksgiving leftovers. The combination of shredded turkey, tangy cranberry sauce, and a blend of cheeses creates a flavorful and festive pizza. The addition of red onion and fresh herbs adds a burst of color and freshness. Feel free to customize the toppings to your liking and enjoy this unique twist on a classic dish.

Turkey and Butternut Squash Tacos

Ingredients:

For the Turkey and Butternut Squash Filling:

- 1 lb ground turkey
- 2 cups butternut squash, diced into small cubes
- 1 tablespoon olive oil
- 1 onion, finely chopped
- 2 cloves garlic, minced
- 1 teaspoon ground cumin
- 1 teaspoon chili powder
- 1/2 teaspoon smoked paprika
- Salt and black pepper, to taste

For the Tacos:

- Soft taco shells or tortillas
- Shredded lettuce
- Diced tomatoes
- Shredded cheese (cheddar or Mexican blend)
- Fresh cilantro, chopped
- Lime wedges
- Salsa or hot sauce (optional)

Instructions:

For the Turkey and Butternut Squash Filling:

> In a large skillet, heat olive oil over medium-high heat.
> Add chopped onion to the skillet and sauté until softened.
> Add minced garlic and diced butternut squash. Cook for about 5 minutes until the squash starts to soften.
> Push the vegetables to the side of the skillet and add ground turkey. Cook until browned, breaking it apart with a spoon as it cooks.
> Stir in ground cumin, chili powder, smoked paprika, salt, and black pepper. Mix well to combine with the turkey and vegetables.
> Cook for an additional 5-7 minutes until the butternut squash is tender, and the turkey is cooked through.

Adjust seasoning if needed and remove from heat.

Assembling the Tacos:

    Warm the soft taco shells or tortillas according to package instructions.
    Spoon the turkey and butternut squash filling onto each taco shell.
    Top with shredded lettuce, diced tomatoes, and shredded cheese.
    Garnish with chopped cilantro and squeeze lime wedges over the tacos.
    Add salsa or hot sauce if desired.
    Serve the Turkey and Butternut Squash Tacos immediately and enjoy this delicious and nutritious twist on traditional tacos!

These Turkey and Butternut Squash Tacos offer a flavorful and hearty filling with a hint of sweetness from the butternut squash. The combination of spices adds depth to the ground turkey, creating a satisfying and well-balanced taco experience. Top them with your favorite fresh toppings for a burst of color and freshness. Perfect for a quick and wholesome weeknight dinner or a festive taco night!

Turkey and Sage Sausage Stuffing

Ingredients:

- 1 pound turkey sausage (sage-flavored if available)
- 8 cups cubed bread (preferably day-old or toasted)
- 1/2 cup unsalted butter
- 1 large onion, finely chopped
- 2 celery stalks, finely chopped
- 3 cloves garlic, minced
- 2 teaspoons dried sage
- 1 teaspoon dried thyme
- 1 teaspoon dried rosemary
- Salt and black pepper, to taste
- 2-3 cups chicken or turkey broth
- Fresh parsley, chopped (for garnish)

Instructions:

Preheat the oven to 350°F (175°C).
In a large skillet, cook the turkey sausage over medium heat, breaking it apart with a spoon as it cooks. Once browned, remove it from the skillet and set it aside.
In the same skillet, melt the butter over medium heat.
Add chopped onion and celery to the skillet. Sauté until the vegetables are softened.
Add minced garlic to the skillet and cook for an additional 1-2 minutes until fragrant.
Stir in the dried sage, thyme, and rosemary. Cook for another minute to release the flavors.
In a large mixing bowl, combine the cubed bread, cooked turkey sausage, and the sautéed vegetable mixture.
Season the mixture with salt and black pepper to taste.
Gradually pour the chicken or turkey broth over the bread mixture, stirring well to moisten the bread evenly. Add enough broth to reach your desired level of moistness.
Transfer the stuffing mixture to a greased baking dish.
Cover the dish with aluminum foil and bake in the preheated oven for 30 minutes.

Remove the foil and bake for an additional 15-20 minutes or until the top is golden brown and crispy.
Garnish with chopped fresh parsley before serving.
Serve the Turkey and Sage Sausage Stuffing as a delicious and savory side dish for your holiday meal!

This Turkey and Sage Sausage Stuffing is a flavorful and aromatic addition to your holiday table. The combination of sage-flavored turkey sausage, herbs, and buttery bread creates a comforting and classic stuffing. The result is a savory side dish that perfectly complements your Thanksgiving or Christmas feast. Enjoy the delicious blend of flavors and textures in every spoonful!

Turkey and Vegetable Kabobs

Ingredients:

For the Marinade:

- 1/4 cup olive oil
- 2 tablespoons soy sauce
- 1 tablespoon Dijon mustard
- 2 cloves garlic, minced
- 1 teaspoon dried oregano
- 1 teaspoon dried thyme
- Salt and black pepper, to taste

For the Kabobs:

- 1.5 lbs turkey breast, cut into cubes
- 1 zucchini, sliced
- 1 bell pepper (any color), cut into chunks
- 1 red onion, cut into chunks
- Cherry tomatoes
- Wooden or metal skewers

Optional Garnish:

- Fresh parsley, chopped

Instructions:

If using wooden skewers, soak them in water for about 30 minutes to prevent burning.

In a bowl, whisk together the olive oil, soy sauce, Dijon mustard, minced garlic, dried oregano, dried thyme, salt, and black pepper to create the marinade.

Place the turkey cubes in a resealable plastic bag or shallow dish. Pour half of the marinade over the turkey, ensuring all pieces are coated. Reserve the other half of the marinade for basting.

Seal the bag or cover the dish and marinate the turkey in the refrigerator for at least 30 minutes to allow the flavors to infuse.

Preheat the grill to medium-high heat.

Thread the marinated turkey cubes, zucchini slices, bell pepper chunks, red onion chunks, and cherry tomatoes onto the skewers, alternating between the ingredients.

Place the kabobs on the preheated grill and cook for about 10-12 minutes, turning occasionally, until the turkey is fully cooked and the vegetables are tender and lightly charred.

During grilling, baste the kabobs with the reserved marinade for added flavor.

Once the turkey is cooked through, remove the kabobs from the grill.

Garnish with chopped fresh parsley if desired.

Serve the Turkey and Vegetable Kabobs warm with your favorite side dishes.

Enjoy this delicious and wholesome grilling recipe that's perfect for a quick and flavorful meal!

These Turkey and Vegetable Kabobs are a fantastic and healthy option for grilling enthusiasts. The marinade adds a savory and herb-infused flavor to the turkey, while the assortment of colorful vegetables brings vibrancy and nutrition to each skewer. Whether served as a main dish or part of a barbecue spread, these kabobs are sure to be a hit. Customize the vegetables based on your preferences and enjoy a delightful meal straight from the grill!

Turkey and Cranberry Croissant Sandwiches

Ingredients:

- 4 large croissants, sliced in half
- 1 pound sliced turkey breast
- 1/2 cup cranberry sauce
- 4 ounces Brie cheese, sliced
- 1 cup baby spinach or arugula
- 1/4 cup mayonnaise
- Salt and black pepper, to taste

Instructions:

Preheat your oven to 350°F (175°C).
Place the croissant halves on a baking sheet and warm them in the preheated oven for about 5 minutes or until they are slightly toasted.
While the croissants are warming, spread a thin layer of mayonnaise on the bottom half of each croissant.
Layer the sliced turkey on the bottom half of each croissant.
Spoon cranberry sauce over the turkey, spreading it evenly.
Place slices of Brie cheese on top of the cranberry sauce.
Season with salt and black pepper to taste.
Add a handful of baby spinach or arugula on top of the Brie.
Place the top half of each croissant on the sandwich to complete it.
Serve the Turkey and Cranberry Croissant Sandwiches immediately, and enjoy the delightful combination of flavors and textures!

These Turkey and Cranberry Croissant Sandwiches are a delicious way to use Thanksgiving leftovers or enjoy a taste of the holiday season any time of the year. The combination of succulent turkey, tangy cranberry sauce, creamy Brie, and fresh greens nestled in a flaky croissant creates a delightful and satisfying sandwich. Whether served for lunch, brunch, or a light dinner, these sandwiches are sure to be a crowd-pleaser!

Turkey and Spinach Frittata

Ingredients:

- 8 large eggs
- 1/2 cup milk
- Salt and black pepper, to taste
- 1 tablespoon olive oil
- 1 small onion, finely chopped
- 2 cloves garlic, minced
- 1 cup cooked turkey, shredded or diced
- 2 cups fresh spinach, chopped
- 1/2 cup feta cheese, crumbled
- 1 tablespoon fresh parsley, chopped (for garnish)

Instructions:

Preheat your oven to the broil setting.
In a bowl, whisk together the eggs, milk, salt, and black pepper until well combined. Set aside.
Heat olive oil in an oven-safe skillet over medium heat.
Add chopped onion and sauté until softened.
Add minced garlic and cook for an additional 1-2 minutes until fragrant.
Add the cooked turkey to the skillet and stir to combine with the onions and garlic.
Stir in the chopped spinach and cook until it wilts.
Pour the egg mixture evenly over the turkey, spinach, and onion mixture in the skillet.
Sprinkle crumbled feta cheese over the top of the frittata.
Cook on the stovetop without stirring for about 3-4 minutes until the edges begin to set.
Transfer the skillet to the preheated oven and broil for 3-5 minutes until the top is set and lightly golden brown.
Remove the frittata from the oven and let it cool slightly.
Garnish with chopped fresh parsley.
Slice the Turkey and Spinach Frittata into wedges and serve warm.
Enjoy this flavorful and protein-packed frittata for breakfast, brunch, or a light dinner!

This Turkey and Spinach Frittata is a versatile and satisfying dish that can be enjoyed for any meal of the day. Packed with protein from the turkey and eggs, and featuring the vibrant flavors of spinach, feta, and fresh herbs, it's a wholesome and delicious option. The broiling step adds a golden finish to the top, making it visually appealing as well. Serve it on its own or with a side salad for a complete and nutritious meal.

Turkey and Green Bean Stir-Fry

Ingredients:

- 1 pound turkey breast or turkey tenderloins, sliced into thin strips
- 1 pound fresh green beans, trimmed and cut into bite-sized pieces
- 2 tablespoons soy sauce
- 1 tablespoon oyster sauce
- 1 tablespoon hoisin sauce
- 1 tablespoon sesame oil
- 2 tablespoons vegetable oil
- 3 cloves garlic, minced
- 1 tablespoon fresh ginger, grated
- 1 red chili, thinly sliced (optional, for heat)
- 2 green onions, sliced
- Sesame seeds, for garnish
- Cooked rice or noodles, for serving

Instructions:

In a small bowl, mix together soy sauce, oyster sauce, hoisin sauce, and sesame oil to create the stir-fry sauce. Set aside.

Heat vegetable oil in a wok or large skillet over high heat.

Add sliced turkey and stir-fry for 2-3 minutes until browned and cooked through. Remove the turkey from the wok and set aside.

In the same wok, add a bit more oil if needed. Add minced garlic, grated ginger, and sliced red chili (if using). Stir-fry for about 30 seconds until fragrant.

Add the green beans to the wok and stir-fry for 3-4 minutes until they are tender-crisp.

Return the cooked turkey to the wok with the green beans.

Pour the stir-fry sauce over the turkey and green beans. Toss everything together until well coated and heated through.

Stir in sliced green onions and cook for an additional 1-2 minutes.

Taste and adjust the seasoning if needed.

Serve the Turkey and Green Bean Stir-Fry over cooked rice or noodles.

Garnish with sesame seeds.

Enjoy this quick and flavorful stir-fry as a delicious and healthy meal!

This Turkey and Green Bean Stir-Fry is a vibrant and nutritious dish that comes together quickly for a delicious weeknight dinner. The combination of tender turkey, crisp green beans, and a flavorful stir-fry sauce creates a well-balanced and satisfying meal. Feel free to customize the vegetables or add your favorite stir-fry ingredients for variety. Serve it over rice or noodles for a complete and wholesome dinner option.

Turkey and Cranberry Wontons

Ingredients:

- 1 cup cooked turkey, finely chopped or shredded
- 1/2 cup cream cheese, softened
- 1/4 cup cranberry sauce
- 1 green onion, finely chopped
- 1 teaspoon soy sauce
- 1/2 teaspoon ginger, grated
- 1 package wonton wrappers
- Water (for sealing wontons)
- Oil (for frying)
- Cranberry sauce, for dipping

Instructions:

In a mixing bowl, combine the chopped turkey, softened cream cheese, cranberry sauce, chopped green onion, soy sauce, and grated ginger. Mix until well combined.
Lay out a wonton wrapper on a clean surface.
Place a small spoonful of the turkey and cream cheese mixture in the center of the wrapper.
Dip your finger in water and moisten the edges of the wrapper.
Fold the wonton in half, creating a triangle, and press the edges to seal.
Repeat the process with the remaining wonton wrappers and filling.
In a deep skillet or fryer, heat oil to 350°F (175°C).
Carefully place the wontons in the hot oil and fry for 2-3 minutes or until golden brown and crispy.
Use a slotted spoon to remove the fried wontons and place them on a paper towel-lined plate to drain excess oil.
Serve the Turkey and Cranberry Wontons warm with cranberry sauce for dipping.
Enjoy this festive and flavorful appetizer for a delightful twist on classic wontons!

These Turkey and Cranberry Wontons are a creative and tasty way to use Thanksgiving leftovers. The combination of savory turkey, creamy cream cheese, and tangy cranberry sauce wrapped in a crispy wonton shell creates a delightful bite-sized appetizer. Whether served as a party snack or a fun finger food for a casual gathering, these wontons are sure to be a hit. Adjust the filling quantities to make as many wontons as desired.

Turkey and Cheddar Stuffed Peppers

Ingredients:

- 4 large bell peppers, halved and seeds removed
- 1 pound ground turkey
- 1 small onion, finely chopped
- 2 cloves garlic, minced
- 1 cup cooked quinoa or rice
- 1 cup black beans, drained and rinsed
- 1 cup corn kernels (fresh or frozen)
- 1 teaspoon ground cumin
- 1 teaspoon chili powder
- Salt and black pepper, to taste
- 1 cup shredded cheddar cheese
- Fresh cilantro, chopped (for garnish)
- Lime wedges (for serving)

Instructions:

Preheat the oven to 375°F (190°C).
Place the halved bell peppers in a baking dish, cut side up.
In a skillet over medium heat, cook the ground turkey until browned. Drain any excess fat.
Add chopped onion and minced garlic to the skillet with the turkey. Sauté until the onion is softened.
Stir in cooked quinoa or rice, black beans, corn, ground cumin, chili powder, salt, and black pepper. Mix well to combine.
Spoon the turkey and quinoa mixture into each bell pepper half.
Top each stuffed pepper with shredded cheddar cheese.
Cover the baking dish with foil and bake in the preheated oven for 25-30 minutes or until the peppers are tender.
Remove the foil and broil for an additional 2-3 minutes until the cheese is melted and bubbly.
Garnish with chopped fresh cilantro.
Serve the Turkey and Cheddar Stuffed Peppers warm with lime wedges on the side.
Enjoy this wholesome and flavorful dish as a satisfying meal!

These Turkey and Cheddar Stuffed Peppers are a nutritious and delicious way to enjoy a classic dish with a twist. The combination of lean ground turkey, quinoa or rice, black beans, and corn creates a well-balanced and protein-packed filling. The melted cheddar cheese on top adds a comforting and cheesy element to each bite. Serve these stuffed peppers for a family-friendly dinner or make them ahead for a convenient and reheatable meal. Customize the filling with your favorite ingredients for added variety!

Turkey and Cranberry Stuffed Acorn Squash

Ingredients:

- 2 acorn squash, halved and seeds removed
- 1 pound ground turkey
- 1 tablespoon olive oil
- 1 small onion, finely chopped
- 2 cloves garlic, minced
- 1 teaspoon dried thyme
- 1 teaspoon dried sage
- Salt and black pepper, to taste
- 1 cup cooked quinoa or rice
- 1/2 cup dried cranberries
- 1/2 cup chopped pecans
- 1/4 cup fresh parsley, chopped
- Feta cheese, crumbled (optional, for garnish)

Instructions:

Preheat the oven to 400°F (200°C).
Place the acorn squash halves, cut side up, on a baking sheet.
Brush the cut sides of the squash with olive oil and sprinkle with salt and black pepper.
Roast in the preheated oven for 30-40 minutes or until the squash is fork-tender.
While the squash is roasting, heat olive oil in a skillet over medium heat.
Add chopped onion and sauté until softened.
Add minced garlic, ground turkey, dried thyme, dried sage, salt, and black pepper. Cook until the turkey is browned and cooked through.
Stir in cooked quinoa or rice, dried cranberries, chopped pecans, and fresh parsley. Cook for an additional 2-3 minutes to heat through.
Once the acorn squash is roasted, fill each half with the turkey and cranberry stuffing mixture.
Optional: Sprinkle crumbled feta cheese over the top for an extra burst of flavor.
Return the stuffed acorn squash to the oven and bake for an additional 10-15 minutes until everything is heated through.
Garnish with additional fresh parsley before serving.
Serve the Turkey and Cranberry Stuffed Acorn Squash warm and enjoy this festive and flavorful dish!

This Turkey and Cranberry Stuffed Acorn Squash is a perfect fall-inspired dish that combines the savory goodness of ground turkey with the sweetness of cranberries and the nuttiness of pecans. The roasted acorn squash serves as a delightful edible bowl for the flavorful stuffing. The addition of feta cheese on top adds a creamy and tangy element. Serve this dish for a comforting and nutritious dinner that captures the essence of the season.

Turkey and Pesto Pasta Salad

Ingredients:

- 8 ounces rotini or your favorite pasta
- 1 pound cooked turkey, shredded or diced
- 1 cup cherry tomatoes, halved
- 1 cup fresh mozzarella balls, halved
- 1/2 cup black olives, sliced
- 1/4 cup pine nuts, toasted
- 1/2 cup fresh basil leaves, chopped
- 1/2 cup grated Parmesan cheese

For the Pesto Dressing:

- 1 cup fresh basil leaves
- 1/2 cup grated Parmesan cheese
- 1/4 cup pine nuts
- 2 cloves garlic, minced
- 1/2 cup extra-virgin olive oil
- Salt and black pepper, to taste
- Juice of 1 lemon

Instructions:

Cook the pasta according to package instructions. Drain and let it cool.
In a blender or food processor, combine fresh basil, grated Parmesan cheese, pine nuts, minced garlic, and lemon juice for the pesto dressing. Blend until smooth.
With the blender or food processor running, slowly stream in the olive oil until the dressing is well combined. Season with salt and black pepper to taste.
In a large bowl, combine the cooked pasta, shredded or diced turkey, cherry tomatoes, mozzarella balls, black olives, and toasted pine nuts.
Pour the pesto dressing over the pasta and turkey mixture. Toss everything together until well coated.
Stir in chopped fresh basil and grated Parmesan cheese.
Refrigerate the Turkey and Pesto Pasta Salad for at least 1 hour to allow the flavors to meld.

Before serving, give the pasta salad a good toss and adjust the seasoning if needed.
Serve the chilled Turkey and Pesto Pasta Salad and enjoy this refreshing and flavorful dish!

This Turkey and Pesto Pasta Salad is a delightful and satisfying dish that combines the savory goodness of turkey with the vibrant flavors of homemade pesto. The pasta, cherry tomatoes, mozzarella, and olives add wonderful textures, while the pesto dressing ties everything together with its herby and zesty notes. Whether served as a side dish or a light main course, this pasta salad is perfect for picnics, potlucks, or a quick and delicious meal.

Turkey and Brussels Sprouts Skillet

Ingredients:

- 1 pound ground turkey
- 1 tablespoon olive oil
- 1 small onion, finely chopped
- 2 cloves garlic, minced
- 1 pound Brussels sprouts, trimmed and halved
- 1 teaspoon dried thyme
- Salt and black pepper, to taste
- 1/2 cup chicken broth
- 1 tablespoon balsamic vinegar
- 1/4 cup grated Parmesan cheese
- Fresh parsley, chopped (for garnish)

Instructions:

In a large skillet, heat olive oil over medium-high heat.
Add ground turkey to the skillet and cook until browned, breaking it apart with a spoon as it cooks. Remove any excess fat.
Add chopped onion and minced garlic to the skillet with the turkey. Sauté until the onion is softened.
Stir in the Brussels sprouts halves and dried thyme. Cook for 5-7 minutes, stirring occasionally, until the Brussels sprouts are golden brown and slightly crispy.
Season with salt and black pepper to taste.
Pour chicken broth and balsamic vinegar into the skillet. Stir to combine, scraping up any browned bits from the bottom of the skillet.
Cover the skillet with a lid and let the Brussels sprouts cook for an additional 5-7 minutes or until they are tender-crisp.
Sprinkle grated Parmesan cheese over the Brussels sprouts and turkey mixture. Stir to combine.
Garnish with chopped fresh parsley before serving.
Taste and adjust the seasoning if needed.
Serve the Turkey and Brussels Sprouts Skillet warm and enjoy this flavorful and nutritious dish!

This Turkey and Brussels Sprouts Skillet is a quick and easy one-pan meal that brings together the lean protein of ground turkey with the vibrant and nutty flavors of Brussels sprouts. The balsamic vinegar adds a delightful tang, and the Parmesan cheese provides a savory and cheesy finish. This dish is not only delicious but also a great way to incorporate more veggies into your meal. Serve it as a wholesome dinner option that's both satisfying and nutritious.

Turkey and Cranberry Empanadas

Ingredients:

For the Dough:

- 2 cups all-purpose flour
- 1/2 teaspoon salt
- 1/2 cup unsalted butter, cold and cut into small cubes
- 1/2 cup cold water

For the Filling:

- 1 pound cooked turkey, shredded or diced
- 1/2 cup cranberry sauce
- 1/2 cup cream cheese, softened
- 1/4 cup green onions, chopped
- Salt and black pepper, to taste

For Assembly:

- 1 egg, beaten (for egg wash)
- Sesame seeds (optional, for garnish)

Instructions:

For the Dough:

In a large bowl, whisk together the flour and salt.
Add the cold, cubed butter to the flour mixture. Use your fingers or a pastry cutter to incorporate the butter until the mixture resembles coarse crumbs.
Gradually add the cold water, mixing until the dough comes together. Form the dough into a ball, wrap it in plastic wrap, and refrigerate for at least 30 minutes.

For the Filling:

In a mixing bowl, combine the cooked turkey, cranberry sauce, cream cheese, and chopped green onions. Season with salt and black pepper to taste. Mix until well combined.

Assembly:

Preheat the oven to 375°F (190°C).
On a floured surface, roll out the chilled dough to about 1/8 inch thickness.
Use a round cutter or a glass to cut out circles from the dough.
Place a spoonful of the turkey and cranberry filling in the center of each dough circle.
Fold the dough over the filling, creating a half-moon shape. Seal the edges by pressing them together with a fork.
Place the empanadas on a baking sheet lined with parchment paper.
Brush the tops of the empanadas with beaten egg and sprinkle with sesame seeds if desired.
Bake in the preheated oven for 15-20 minutes or until the empanadas are golden brown.
Allow the Turkey and Cranberry Empanadas to cool slightly before serving.
Enjoy these festive and flavorful empanadas as a delightful appetizer or snack!

These Turkey and Cranberry Empanadas are a delicious and creative way to use leftover turkey, especially during the holiday season. The combination of tender turkey, sweet cranberry sauce, and creamy cream cheese wrapped in a flaky pastry creates a delightful handheld treat. Serve them as an appetizer for holiday gatherings or enjoy them as a tasty snack. The sesame seed garnish adds a subtle crunch to each bite.

Turkey and Cranberry Hand Pies

Ingredients:

For the Dough:

- 2 cups all-purpose flour
- 1/2 teaspoon salt
- 1 cup unsalted butter, cold and cut into small cubes
- 1/2 cup cold water

For the Filling:

- 2 cups cooked turkey, shredded or diced
- 1/2 cup cranberry sauce
- 1/4 cup cream cheese, softened
- 1/4 cup green onions, chopped
- Salt and black pepper, to taste

For Assembly:

- 1 egg, beaten (for egg wash)
- Sesame seeds (optional, for garnish)

Instructions:

For the Dough:

In a large bowl, whisk together the flour and salt.
Add the cold, cubed butter to the flour mixture. Use your fingers or a pastry cutter to incorporate the butter until the mixture resembles coarse crumbs.
Gradually add the cold water, mixing until the dough comes together. Form the dough into a ball, wrap it in plastic wrap, and refrigerate for at least 30 minutes.

For the Filling:

In a mixing bowl, combine the cooked turkey, cranberry sauce, cream cheese, and chopped green onions. Season with salt and black pepper to taste. Mix until well combined.

Assembly:

Preheat the oven to 375°F (190°C).
On a floured surface, roll out the chilled dough to about 1/8 inch thickness.
Use a round cutter or a glass to cut out circles from the dough.
Place a spoonful of the turkey and cranberry filling in the center of each dough circle.
Fold the dough over the filling, creating a half-moon shape. Seal the edges by pressing them together with a fork.
Place the hand pies on a baking sheet lined with parchment paper.
Brush the tops of the hand pies with beaten egg and sprinkle with sesame seeds if desired.
Bake in the preheated oven for 15-20 minutes or until the hand pies are golden brown.
Allow the Turkey and Cranberry Hand Pies to cool slightly before serving.
Enjoy these handheld delights as a festive and flavorful appetizer or snack!

These Turkey and Cranberry Hand Pies are a delightful and convenient way to enjoy the flavors of a holiday meal in a handheld form. The combination of tender turkey, sweet cranberry sauce, and creamy cream cheese encased in a flaky pastry creates a perfect bite-sized treat. Serve them as a festive appetizer or enjoy them as a portable snack during the holiday season. The sesame seed garnish adds a subtle crunch to each hand pie.

www.ingramcontent.com/pod-product-compliance
Lightning Source LLC
LaVergne TN
LVHW081556060526
838201LV00054B/1921